FROGMAN
SPY

FROGMAN SPY

The mysterious disappearance of
Commander 'Buster' Crabb

M.G. and J.A. Welham

W H ALLEN

First published in Great Britain 1990
by W.H. Allen & Co Plc
Sekforde House, 175–9 St John Street,
London EC1V 4LL

© M.G. and J.A. Welham 1990

ISBN 1-85227-138-8

Typeset by Avocet Robinson, Buckingham
Printed and bound in Great Britain by
Mackays of Chatham Plc, Chatham, Kent

Dedicated to
Dr V. Svoboda
and his
medical staff

Contents

Authors' Note

Former mole-hunting MI5 officer Peter Wright declares that Sir Roger Hollis, Director-General of MI5 in the 1950s, was a Soviet spy.

Nigel West, in his book *Molehunt*, claims that it was not Hollis but Graham Mitchell, the Deputy Director-General, who was, in fact, the spy.

The era uncovered Soviet spies in the secret services and in due course the names of Burgess, Maclean, Philby and Blunt became generally known. But one Soviet spy remained and operated at a very high level.

Operations for the British secret services did not go well during this period. This is the story of one man and his secret service mission who was betrayed by the KGB's master spy.

Acknowledgements

The authors wish to express their sincere thanks to the following, whose assistance has been invaluable in the preparation of this book: the Belloni family; Bild Newspapers (Germany); Broadland Investigations (Norwich); the Crabb family; the Czechoslovakians; Norman Dean; Frank Goldsworthy, former journalist and Naval Intelligence officer; Siebe Gorman; Sydney Knowles; Maria Visintini Montella; NTS; Maitland Pendock's son; Mike O'Meara; the late Pat Rose; Bruce Quarrie.

Special thanks go also to those who have provided information but who either must or wish to remain anonymous, and to those whose assistance and advice has been of great value but who are not named individually.

1

Hot Potato

Spy stories often feature agents who are told when they go on a mission that, if anything goes wrong, they will be 'on their own' and disowned by their government. Similarly, in real life, many governments frown publicly on mercenaries and spies, but behind the scenes actively aid and abet their missions, fully intending to deny all knowledge in the event of a foul-up. Occasionally, however, things go wrong and the press gets wind of a story. When that happens cover-ups are rarely successful, and when the truth emerges all hell is let loose. Watergate is one such example.

One British government cover-up has been sustained for thirty years, with only a few people outside the bureaucracy knowing the real truth, and these so intimidated by the Official Secrets Act or other pressure that they have kept quiet . . . until now, that is. The mysterious disappearance of wartime hero 'Buster' Crabb in 1956 became something of a *cause célèbre* and, despite various efforts over the years by a number of writers to get at the truth, only now can the duplicity of Sir Anthony Eden's and successive governments – both Conservative and Labour – be revealed.

Commander Lionel Kenneth Philip Crabb, GM, OBE, RNVR, nicknamed 'Buster' by the popular press (although it was a title he detested and which those who knew him never used), first became known to the public during the Second World War when his exploits as an underwater demolitions expert, or 'frogman', came to light. After the war he was involved in further underwater adventures, described later in this book, which kept him newsworthy. When he disappeared, ostensibly during an operation which the Admiralty clumsily tried to pass off as routine testing of new equipment, questions were inevitably asked. The speculation was exacerbated by the fact that a modern Russian cruiser, the *Ordzhonikidze*, was visiting Portsmouth at the time, carrying Premier Khrushchev and Marshal Bulganin on a goodwill visit to Britain. What *was* Crabb doing that April morning in the murky water of Portsmouth harbour?, the media asked. The obvious answer was that he was conducting an underwater examination of the Soviet ship's hull to discover what secrets this might reveal; but he had in fact already done this when the cruiser's sister ship *Sverdlov* had visited Portsmouth the previous year, thereby disclosing the secret of her manoeuvrability.

Questions were asked in the House, of course, not least because the Russians had lodged an official complaint about the presence of a frogman near their ships. Finally, on 9 May, the then Prime Minister Sir Anthony Eden baldly told a packed House of Commons that 'It would not be in the public interest to disclose the circumstances in which Commander Crabb is presumed to have met his death.'

Hugh Gaitskell, the leader of the Opposition, told the Prime Minister that his statement was totally unsatisfactory, and asked whether he was aware that, 'while all of us would wish to protect public security, the suspicion must inevitably arise that his refusal to make a statement on this subject is not so much in the interest of public security as to hide a very grave blunder which has occurred' From that day to this no prime minister of any political party, nor any other government official, has said any more about the affair than that Commander Crabb was presumed drowned while conducting experimental tests with new equipment and it would not be in the public interest to discuss it.

That was thirty years ago, and any 'secret equipment' tested would long since have featured in the pages of *Jane's* and other reference books, so why the continued veil of secrecy? The fact that Cabinet papers released to the public at the beginning of 1987 under the 'thirty-year rule' reveal Eden's deception of the government and the country over British involvement at Suez, but make no mention of Crabb (the relevant papers are locked away for further decades), would seem to be strong evidence of a cover-up at the highest level.

Our quest for the truth began one day in London's Imperial War

Museum. Looking through photographs as part of a completely unrelated research project, we kept coming across pictures of one particular individual, Commander Crabb. He was described to us by a member of the museum staff, who claimed to have known him, as 'an objectionable little man' – a strange remark in itself since we subsequently discovered that, although Crabb was something of a loner, all his friends were fiercely loyal and gave an impression of someone who was well liked as well as admired for his courage. However, the museum official made a parting remark which fired our curiosity. 'He was involved in that Russian ship business at Portsmouth. Some say he went to Russia.' Little did we then suspect that these seeds of idle curiosity would grow into an obsession.

Our first task was to obtain every book that had been written about Crabb, both during the war and afterwards. The initial impression we received from these books was of a man apparently rejected by the Royal Navy who still sought to maintain the appearance of an adventurer; there was also a strong indication of covert espionage. Both images eventually formed part of the truth, but we trod a long and hard road to prove them. To this day some pieces of the jigsaw remain lost.

There have been many theories explaining the need for Crabb's dive. In *Commander Crabb is Alive*, Bernard Hutton states that the CIA and the Admiralty were keen to find out why the *Ordzhonikidze*, was so manoeuvrable, and this was in fact the reason for Crabb's dive under the *Sverdlov*. A bizarre story was told by Harry Houghton in his book *Operation Portland*, which stated that Crabb had to swim under the cruiser with a special limpet mine. The mine was to be placed near the ship's ASDIC (sonar) dome. If the Russians had the technology to produce a new type of ASDIC, it would transmit on a certain impulse, which would detonate the mine. The mine's explosive impact would not cause any serious injury, merely enough damage to slow the ship down, which would have been observed by the Navy. If the ASDIC was not of the new type, the mine would have dropped off after three days. But it is hard to believe that one Naval power would place an explosive device upon another warship during a friendly visit.

In *Too Secret Too Long*, Chapman Pincher explains that naval intelligence wanted to discover whether the ship was fitted with an anti-sonar device, code-named 'Agouti'. The aim of the device was to decrease the cavitation effects produced by the screws so as to reduce underwater noise. This type of operation was usually undertaken by underwater listening devices and by submarines monitoring the ship's signature. It is most doubtful that a diver would be used for such a task.

Another theory is put forward in *Burgess and Maclean*, a book by John Fisher, which states that Crabb was looking for a hatch from which the ship could lay nuclear mines. And one report stated that Crabb was carrying an underwater camera and was electrocuted by its power cable, although it would have been totally impossible to drag a cable across a debris-littered seabed, or to handle a bulky 1950s camera underwater.

But the principal questions which have been asked by everybody having any knowledge of the Crabb affair are: did Crabb die in the filth of Portsmouth harbour beneath the Russian leader's ship – or was he captured and whisked back to the Soviet Union? If he was killed, or if he had suffered an equipment failure and died, it would have been embarrassing to the powers that be, but no more than that. Perhaps, therefore, he had been captured and the story of his death was a cover-up. But why? At 46 Crabb was past his prime and drank and smoked quite heavily. He had *officially* left the Navy and was working as a furniture salesman at the time of his 'disappearance'. For what possible purpose would the Russians want to snatch him?

We had an advantage in trying to explore the subject – or so we thought. One of us (Mike) had been a diver in the Royal Marines and knew personally many of the naval diving personnel who had been around at the time of Crabb's disappearance. We telephoned an old friend whom we had not seen for some time, and after the usual pleasantries asked whether he had been in Portsmouth in 1956. He agreed, guardedly, that he had, but when asked what he knew about the Crabb affair he clammed up. Though we pointed out that the whole incident was nearly thirty years in the past, he insisted that he could say nothing. His exact words were that if 'they' could trace the source of the information, it would be 'more than my life's worth'.

The man to whom we were talking was no ordinary chap. He had been decorated for dealing with bombs and mines while with the Naval

Clearance Diving Branch. He was, therefore, no coward. But on this subject he was as coy as a schoolgirl on her first date, and warned us that the whole subject was covered by the Official Secrets Act and was so 'dangerous' that we would have to watch ourselves. It was only later that we learned that other people who had got too close to the truth of the Crabb affair had died or disappeared under very mysterious circumstances.

At the time, however, the warning did not put us off. We managed to get in touch with a mutual friend of the man we had first telephoned, who lives abroad but was coincidentally visiting Britain shortly after we wrote. We had a traditional Sunday lunch in a pub in the heart of the countryside, but the conversation was anything but traditional. Our friend, who for reasons which will become obvious had to remain anonymous, first warned that the whole subject of Crabb's disappearance was still covered by the Official Secrets Act. Appreciating the seriousness of this we readily agreed to conceal our friend's identity, but nevertheless went straight to the point: was there more to the story than the fanciful press reports about a reconnaissance mission beneath the Soviet cruiser indicated?

Our friend was reluctant to answer. However he did volunteer the information that, whatever Crabb had been up to, it was not a job organised by the Royal Navy, and that he had been wearing the Italian diving gear he favoured rather than RN issue. Curiouser and curiouser . . . Was Crabb in possession of any information which would have been useful to the Russians? That our friend found difficult to say, though we were to discover the answer later.

We then enquired about the body.

No less than fourteen months after Crabb disappeared a macabre corpse, dressed in diving gear of Italian make identical to that which Crabb habitually used, but lacking both a head and hands, had been fished ashore near Chichester, on the English south coast and not that far away from Portsmouth. An inquest had declared it to be Crabb's body, but there were anomalies about the inquest itself and firm evidence, quoted later, proves it to have been rigged by men with official credentials powerful enough to intimidate both coroner and witnesses. Moreover, when the body was buried in Portsmouth, Crabb's mother caused a very strange headstone to be erected over it, which eventually proved a key piece in the jigsaw puzzle. In the pub on that day, however, all our friend would say was that he had 'nearly' been called upon to identify the body. He was still in the Navy at the time, but close to retirement. He said that the reason he had not been called upon as a witness was because of that very fact, for the authorities wanted witnesses who still had a full active career ahead of them, and would therefore be more securely bound by the Official Secrets Act. 'I suppose they could keep control over the situation better,' he said. 'Those in higher places, you know.' Even then, our friend would not say whether or not he thought the body buried at Portsmouth was Crabb's, and there the conversation ended.

We now had a compounded mystery on our hands. The official line was that Crabb had disappeared, presumed drowned, while undertaking tests on secret new naval equipment. The press view was that he had died or been killed while snooping beneath the cruiser *Ordzhonikidze*, or had been kidnapped and ferried back to Russia. There was even more speculation, though Crabb was always first and foremost a patriot, that he had defected. But if he had been kidnapped, or had defected, then whose was the body washed up at Chichester? The more questions were raised, the more determined we became to arrive at the truth.

We soon found that this was going to be far from easy. People either refused to say anything, or those interested in the affair themselves wanted to trade information for what we already knew: with neither side knowing what information the other had, we had to move through the Crabb 'minefield' with great care. Another problem, of course, was that the incident had occurred thirty years earlier, and people's memories had dimmed.

Then we had two strokes of good fortune. We managed to locate Patricia Rose, Crabb's fiancée, who had been one of the last people to see him before his disappearance. Although she was ill with cancer (and has subsequently died) she agreed to help us and her information gradually convinced us that Crabb had, indeed, been captured by Soviet sailors from the *Ordzhonikidze* and taken back to Russia. The second stroke of luck was in finding Sydney Knowles, one of Crabb's oldest friends from the war and, moreover, the man who had accompanied Crabb during his underwater inspection of the hull of the cruiser *Sverdlov* in 1955. Even more importantly, Knowles had been called upon to 'identify' the body washed up at Chichester. His evidence, quoted later, is both devastating and damning.

There remained the puzzle as to why the Russians should want to capture a 46-year-old retired naval diver. The answer lies in the sinister-sounding *Spetsnaz* organisation. At the end of the Second World War the Soviet Navy began taking a great interest in the exploits of the British and Italians who had pioneered underwater warfare techniques, as free-swimming frogmen, as charioteers on human torpedoes and as the crews of miniature submarines. The fact that such men were also fully trained in harbour demolition work and in underwater bomb and mine disposal was also significant to the Russians, who largely lacked such experts of their own or experience in this area.

Spetsnaz or, to give it its full title, *Vyska Spetsial Nogo Naznachenniya*, is the Soviet equivalent of the British Special Air Service Regiment and Special Boat Squadron, or the American SEALs and Green Berets, specially trained and equipped for both covert and overt operations behind enemy lines. In the 1950s it was little more than an idea, but by the 1980s *Spetsnaz* had grown to be a force to reckon with and is equipped, amongst other hi-tech pieces of kit, with miniature submarines which can be released from a mother ship outside territorial limits and which can crawl up to the shore along the sea bed on tracks, like tanks. The full scope of *Spetsnaz* has long been one of the Soviet Union's most closely guarded secrets, and the West had little knowledge of its extent or operational role until the defection of Victor Suvorov, a highly placed Army officer in the GRU (*Glavnoye Razvedyvatelnoye Upravleniye*, or military intelligence). Further details are given in a later chapter; at this juncture it is enough to say that, in 1956, a man of Crabb's calibre, knowledge and experience would have been invaluable to the Soviet Navy in building up their *Spetsnaz* underwater teams.

Crabb, however, would never have voluntarily gone to work for a foreign power and potential enemy of Britain. To those who knew him, the idea of Commander Crabb defecting was, and still is, ludicrous. But all the evidence pointed to Crabb not only being alive, but working under an assumed name as a commissioned officer in the Soviet Navy throughout the 1960s and '70s. Other pieces of evidence now began to drop into place. If the Soviet Navy wanted someone like Crabb as an instructor, British and American intelligence would have been equally keen to place someone with his qualities of observation and his knowledge of underwater equipment and techniques inside this new and ominous *Spetsnaz* organisation. The conclusion is that MI6 and the CIA conceived a joint operation to persuade the Russians that Crabb was a potential defector, and then place him in a situation where he could easily be captured. This could explain why he became a disgruntled furniture salesman, apparently abandoned by the Royal Navy and somewhat bitter. It might also explain the fact that his name nevertheless appears in the Navy Lists for both 1955 and 1956.

Unfortunately for Crabb, who would have been expecting to be pulled out of Russia after he had learned all he could about *Spetsnaz*, British intelligence – and particularly naval intelligence – was riddled with Soviet spies, as has since been discovered. The Soviet authorities would have known about the whole scheme in advance. They would have been delighted to play along, of course, using Crabb for their own purposes but making very sure that any rescue bid would fail. Eventually Crabb would have been told the truth, that he had been abandoned by the faceless men who persuaded him to undertake the mission, and he would have been given two alternatives: continue to cooperate, or be shot as a spy. Faced with the fact that he had been really 'left out in the cold', Crabb would have had no choice but to cooperate. And by that time he would have had such detailed knowledge of *Spetsnaz* that he could never be part of an exchange deal.

So where is Crabb now? The quest took us behind the Iron Curtain as well as to Italy, and ultimately back to that cemetery in Portsmouth where the body found at Chichester was buried. It led us down many strange paths, through which we gained access and insight into many things which could not be known in the 1950s or, indeed, until the 1980s.

Another writer once posed this hypothetical question to a group of military students: are a thousand men imprisoned by an enemy sufficient reason to go to war? The answer was 'yes'. If a thousand men are sufficient reason, he then asked, is one? After a pause, the answer again came back 'yes'. By analogy, the instructor said, you are claiming that a single potato is worth exactly the same as a thousand potatoes. 'No, sir,' said a student. 'Men are not potatoes.'

To successive British governments, however, Commander Crabb has been a 'hot potato' which they have not wished to handle, and this poses a very important question which helps explain why we have decided the truth behind the Crabb affair must emerge. In a free society such as Britain the issue of a man's fate must be fundamental, and the abandonment of Commander Crabb to save intelligence agencies embarrassment should never have been allowed to happen.

2

The Italians

Lioria Visintini was the most idolised man in the Italian underwater assault group. It was 19 September 1941, and his plan was to force his way under the defensive anti-submarine steel net at Gibraltar's harbour entrance. Aboard his chariot he carried compressed air cutters and lifting gear, but he was lucky for the net was lowered to allow a destroyer to pass and he was able to slip through in its wake. He left his chariot's warhead beneath a tanker, forced his way under the net he had passed earlier and got away.

Visintini made the Spanish coast and joined his equally successful companions. A cloud of smoke inside the harbour at Gibraltar announced that his charge had broken the back of the naval tanker *Denbydale*. Soon after there were similar explosions below the 10,900-ton cargo ship *Durham* and the 2,444-ton storage tanker *Fiona Shell* in the bay.

The Royal Navy at Gibraltar were not idle after the attack. At irregular intervals, searchlights swept the harbour approaches, combined with harbour and bay controls. Around the entrance gate, small explosive charges, sufficient to kill or stun a person underwater, were thrown into the water every few minutes of the night. The most significant move of all was the creation of the Gibraltar naval diving party, whose members were to show no less devotion, endurance and courage than their Italian adversaries. This was to expose one member of the party to newspaper headlines, long after the Second World War was finished, and would also enable him to forge strong links with his former 'enemies'.

In 1942, Lieutenant Lionel Crabb, RNVR (Special Branch), took up

the duties of principal mine and bomb disposal officer in Gibraltar.*
His superior officer was Commander Ralph Hancock, who was in
command of minesweeping and extended defences. During the meeting
when Crabb was briefed on his duties, he was informed of the exploits
of the Italian underwater attackers against the shipping berthed in the
Gibraltar area. He was told of the work undertaken by the naval
underwater working party, whose role was to search the undersides of
ships and recover any mines or warheads they found. Hancock explained
that, when the divers found a device, they would remove it and bring
it to the surface where it would become Crabb's responsibility to dispose
of it.

Crabb reflected on the huge task of searching the undersides of ships
in deep water, in all weathers and during day or night, never knowing
when a mine might explode. There must, he decided, be a large and
highly trained underwater party for such a task, and ventured to ask
Hancock how many divers were available. 'Two,' was the astonishing
reply. 'They are not professional divers, they are not mine disposal
people and they have no proper diving gear!'.

Even though he was not a strong swimmer, Crabb decided it was his
duty to learn to dive himself in order that he could do his assigned job
more effectively. He introduced himself to the two divers, Lieutenant
Bailey and Leading Seaman Bell, and soon discovered what 'no proper
diving gear' meant. Instead of the protective rubber suits used by the
Italians, all they had were swimming trunks and overalls; instead of
flippers, they wore plimsolls; and instead of proper diving masks and
breathing apparatus, they had 'scrounged' Davis Submarine Escape
Apparatus (DSEA) designed to help submariners escape a sunken boat.

With some trepidation, Crabb ventured into the water for his first
dive, tethered by a rope held by Bailey in case he got into difficulty.
After this, Bailey escorted him on an inspection of a ship's hull, then
the two men celebrated Crabb's 'graduation' with a drink.

*NB. For most details of Crabb's wartime exploits we must acknowledge the huge
debt owed to Marshall Pugh, his official biographer who began writing his book
before Crabb's disappearance (*Commander Crabb*, Macmillan, 1956). However,
our account also includes information specifically given to us by both Sydney
Knowles and Frank Goldsworthy, a former correspondent for the *Daily Express*
who followed Crabb's career closely.

Meanwhile Visintini, seeking new ways of attacking the ships in Gibraltar, came up with the idea of making a human torpedo base inside the *Olterra*, one of two Italian tankers detained in British contraband control anchorage in Gibraltar bay when Italy entered the war. A few minutes before the declaration of war, both ships' captains received secret radio signals to scuttle their vessels, and both ships were later towed to Algeciras harbour. In 1942, the *Olterra* was lying at a lonely breakwater berth just inside the harbour entrance.

Under Visintini's direction, the Italians cut a 25-foot-long section in the steel bulkhead separating the bow compartment from a small cargo hold, and hinged it like a coffee stall front. Then, telling the Spanish 'neutrality' guard that they must clean the trimming tanks, they pumped out the forward tanks till the bows rose high out of the water.

Early one morning, while the brandy-soaked security guard was sound asleep in the galley, a four-foot door was cut in the side of the ship, opening into the bow compartment six feet below the normal water line. It was hinged to open inwards and so neatly done that only a diver could have detected it. When the ship resumed her normal trim, the bow compartment was flooded but the hold was still dry.

The plan was to sling human torpedoes on pulleys in the bow compartment. When night came for an attack, they could be lowered into the water, pass out of the ship through the door in the side, do their job and return to the secret base. The next part of the plan was to secretly bring through Spain the human torpedoes and the 500lb warheads disguised as parts needed for an engine overhaul. This done, the team was ready for the next attack.

On the night of 7–8 December 1942, Visintini stood on the bridge of the ship with his team and pointed out the silhouettes of two battleships and two aircraft carriers of Force H inside Gibraltar harbour, three miles away. They left the safety of the *Olterra* and began their attack. It took them several hours to reach the harbour approaches, and all the time they could hear through the water the thud of small charges exploding by the harbour gate. They had to gamble on getting through between charges. Visintini and his companion, Petty Officer Magro, paid with their lives, killed by the explosive charges dropped at the gate their bodies were found inside the harbour two weeks later. Two other members of the team were captured and one drowned, so that night the Italians had lost five men and gained nothing.

Visintini and Magro were buried at sea with naval honours. Crabb managed to find two Italian flags and a priest to officiate. There was one wreath, which was thrown on the sea by Crabb and Bailey, the British officers whose task it had been, on that night, to search the ships' bottoms after the attack – knowing that at any moment a warhead explosion within half a mile might kill or maim them. It was a generous gesture much misunderstood and criticised by others at Gibraltar.

The underwater war continued, with the Italians attacking and Crabb's team defending. But it was becoming more difficult for the attackers and they were subjected to greater losses, often without even gaining access to a target. Eventually Gibraltar was considered too well defended and the attacks ceased. For Crabb it was the end of one era and the beginning of another. His exploits in underwater warfare had already earned him the George Medal.

Lieutenant Crabb was promoted to Lieutenant Commander in the summer of 1944 and ordered to select one of his divers and proceed to Italy. He chose Sydney Knowles, who had joined the Gibraltar team in 1943, and they departed the now quieter Gibraltar to join the Joint Services Intelligence Collecting Unit which was based in Florence. The mines that Crabb and his team had been disarming were produced there and he soon became an authority on the mines, warheads and operations of the Italian Tenth Light Flotilla. Crabb had waged his war against this unit and was now carrying that fight into their homeland.

In Florence Crabb and Knowles teamed up with Lieutenant Tony Marsloe, an American of Italian descent who, as a member of the USNR, was a trained intelligence officer and spoke Italian. One of their first tasks was to interrogate a former Italian naval officer from the Tenth Flotilla who had joined the partisans fighting the Germans after Italy's surrender. He provided details of a new type of mine which would cause the divers a great deal of problems when they tried to disarm or remove it. He also stated that pro-German members of the Tenth Flotilla had regrouped and would continue their underwater attacks against captured ports and the Allied ships in them. This was news to British Naval Headquarters who decided to pull Crabb (and his team) away from the Intelligence Collecting Unit and give him the job of supervising anti-sabotage diving operations in the whole Allied-controlled northern part of Italy.

Crabb and Knowles moved to Leghorn (Livorno) where they were joined for diving operations by another Italian, Ventiorini, who became a stalwart member of the team. Command of all anti-sabotage diving in northern Italy was a monumental risk, but Crabb was fortunate when other members of the Tenth Flotilla joined them. Those who joined him found an understanding leader, for he allowed his prisoners considerable freedom, often against the wishes of his superiors.

After two months in hospital with jaundice, Crabb rejoined his team in March 1945. Also immediately, Tony Marsloe discovered from the partisans that the Republicans of the Tenth Flotilla had set up a base for training Italian and German frogmen in the use of human torpedoes on the small island of La Vignole. It was no longer operational, but was guarded by two sergeants who refused to surrender to the communist-led partisans for fear that their valuable equipment would ultimately fall into Russian hands. Crabb and Marsloe were, however, able to secure the base and the services of the two sergeants.

Crabb learned from these men that the partisans had a very important prisoner in the form of Commander Angelo Belloni, who had designed much of the Italian diving equipment used during the war. In fact it was he who had persuaded Mussolini to form the Tenth Flotilla. Crabb negotiated to have him released, and Belloni joined the growing underwater work group. Belloni had two daughters, Minella and Paola, and the latter joined them to help with secretarial work.

Sidney Knowles recalls that 'Paola's sister Minella ended up marrying our number two, Tony Marsloe. We all thought that Crabb and Paola would marry, it was like that, they were close. It was strange, I've never known why they didn't marry, one of the things that never happened, but I believe that they met again after the war, in England, and Crabbie went to Italy. He had little time for women,' Syd continued, 'but I don't mean anything by that. It was just that there were not many divers, and we were kept very busy.' Nevertheless, it may well have been his relationship with Paola that encouraged him to change his religion, for he became devoted to Italy and its people and a devout convert to the Catholic faith.

Crabb, as the principal diving officer in the area of northern Italy, was next ordered to secure Venice from mines and to open the port to Allied shipping. He was faced with the largest mine clearing task of his career. His command included Tony Marsloe as his number two, Angelo Belloni in charge of equipment, a doctor and other divers. They were very successful, even devising measures against magnetic mines which could be set off by the presence of their metal air tanks, as described in Marshall Pugh's biography, *Commander Crabb* (Macmillan, 1956).

With the war ended, Crabb personally accepted the surrender of one of the Tenth Flotilla's leaders, Lieutenant Eugenio Wolk, who had continued to fight the Allies, both working with and training the Germans. Now he was to lead many men of his former unit in searching for those German mines. Technically he was a prisoner, but he was a prisoner who went home to his wife and family in the evening. He often stated that his men never carried arms and that the limpet mines were too small to endanger the crews of the ships. 'Only our own lives were in danger,' was his argument. He had forgotten the British naval divers who had made it their business to seek and remove the charges. Yet when the day came for him to be judged for his anti-Allied work, after the Armistice, one letter saved him his liberty and his civil rights: it came from Lieutenant Commander Crabb.

It was Wolk who arranged the introduction of Crabb to Maria Visintini, the widow of the diver Crabb had buried at sea off Gibraltar. Crabb and Wolk called upon Maria Visintini, who wanted to hear how her husband had died and been buried. The young woman he met was blonde and attractive, despite being dressed in mourning black for her husband. Although she said little, Maria had a profound effect on Crabb and, as she spoke some English and had secretarial experience, he considered offering her a job. Wolk was not over-enthusiastic about the idea but, a few days later, Crabb was told that Maria Visintini had come to see him. She had written a letter which Wolk asked Crabb to read before he saw her. In it she expressed her appreciation for his concern and her desire to work for him. One of the most poignant passages in her letter read: 'Now everything is dead and it is very strange that I'm speaking so just with you. May I think to be rightly understood by you? Life goes on. One must go on with life trying to be plucky and honest. Heart is a secret precious thing that can be seen by nobody.

I need working. My husband's spirit from his heaven of peace sees in my heart and he can't but approve me. (This for your peace of mind.) My pride and his was, is to show how much Italian people can value. This is my strength and my consolation. (And this is the promise for my well to do work.) Now I'm very grateful for you to give me the possibility of work among you rather than otherwhere and so I've come to hear your conditions.'

Crabb read the letter several times before inviting her into the office and asking her to become his secretary. She accepted, and turned out to be very efficient as well.

In December 1945 Crabb was ordered to Naples with his diving equipment, where he was briefed on a new job – helping overcome the terrorist bomb problem in Palestine where militant Jews were trying to expel the British in order to establish their own homeland. British ships and police launches were prime targets, and teams of frogmen made limpet mine attacks against them. Crabb's task, therefore, was to go to Palestine and establish an underwater bomb and mine disposal working party. He had only just arrived in the country when he was awarded the OBE for his work in Italy. The task of the team was that of searching the undersides of ships as they had done so many times before in Gibraltar and Italy. It was not until the spring of 1947 that Crabb was finally ordered home, and a year later he walked out of a demobilisation centre in Portsmouth with a cardboard box, which held a grey chalk-stripe flannel suit.

3

The Post War Years

Crabb first met Patricia Rose* when she was sunk in depression, for she had lost her first husband in 1945 when, as a pilot in Coastal Command, he was shot down in the sea and never found. She then met Peter Aitken, the son of Lord Beaverbrook, and fell in love with him. Whilst his divorce was going through he decided to get away on a sailing holiday. He fell overboard and was drowned. Pat was now close to taking her own life.

Dressed in a flattering blue suit, she went out to the Nag's Head pub in Kinnerton Street, Knightsbridge, where she knew the landlord, Len Cole. Whilst she spoke to people she knew Len poured her a glass of champagne. She told Len that he was very generous, only to be told that it was from Commander Crabb. She saw the small man who raised a glass in salute and approached her. 'To the most beautiful girl in the world, whom I have loved for years.' Pat Rose thought he was quite

*The events described here and later by Pat Rose are as told to us shortly before her death. They do conflict in detail with information related in the late Bernard Hutton's two books, *Commander Crabb is Alive* (Tandem, 1968) and *The Fake Defector* (Howard Baker, 1970). Hutton was very close to Pat Rose and his pioneering work in uncovering at least part of the truth behind Crabb's 'disappearance' has been essential in helping us follow up our own leads. It is probable that Hutton's verbatim accounts of, for example, the journey to Portsmouth (see later) are more accurate than Pat Rose's subsequent recollections when we spoke to her, but the important ingredients remain the same. Similarities in wording and phraseology are inevitable because Pat had told the story so many times before, and any apparent plagiarism of Bernard Hutton's books in these respects is due to this fact alone.

mad, but instantly liked him. They left the Nag's Head and went to the nightclub Churchill's, in Bond Street, where she soon forgot all thoughts of suicide. A dozen red roses arrived at her front door the next day, sealing the friendship.

Crabb was assigned an overseas posting but first he asked Pat to marry him. She was flattered, but explained that it was all too quick. He would be away, and she had not got over her past associations. He then asked if they could get engaged and she agreed. The day Crabbie received his George Medal they became engaged and celebrated at the Cavendish Hotel which was owned by Rosa Lewis of 'The Duchess of Duke Street' fame. Crabb's mother, several fellow officers and Pat Rose's brother were present. He gave her a diamond and ruby ring. Rosa was the queen of the party and knew Crabb well, for they had been friends for years. She toasted them: 'Here's to the Admiral and Lady Hamilton' – the titles by which they were affectionately nicknamed.

Crabb now found himself involved in developing a new kind of underwater filming whilst employed by the Admiralty on secret diving work. A civilian working for the Navy, he was in his own words to be a sort of honorary civil servant. It was because of his vast experience of working underwater that the Admiralty, through its many diverse channels, continued to utilise his services. He prepared for a foreign tour where he was to film naval clearance divers as they disposed of bombs and mines. Whilst waiting to depart on 12 January 1950 he heard the news that a Swedish motor ship, the *Divina*, whilst making its way into the Thames estuary, had collided with an object. The crew could not identify anything or any persons in the water.

Details were soon released when survivors were rescued by another vessel. The *Divina* had collided with HM Submarine *Truculent*. Fifteen men, including the Captain, had been rescued but 64 men were still trapped below. Crabb, accompanied by another diver, Jimmy Hodges, promptly set off for Sheerness with his diving gear.

The stricken submarine lay in shallow water but the strength of the current in the estuary made diving difficult. According to the survivors she had flooded rapidly following the collision, and much of her escape equipment was in the flooded forward compartments. Ten men managed to escape using the few Davis Submarine Escape Apparatus sets remaining, but over twenty others who made the attempt were simply swept out to sea by the current, to drown or die of exposure.

Crabb and Hodges decided to attempt a dive to try and ascertain whether there were any more survivors aboard. To give themselves a lifeline they dragged their motor boat's anchor along the bottom until it caught on the submarine, then Crabb descended. However, the combination of the current and the dark murky water defeated him, as it did Hodges when he made an attempt. They decided they would have to wait for the slack tide.

On the second attempt Crabb and Hodges reached the submarine and tapped their way along the hull, listening intently for any reply. There was none. Then Crabb hit a snag: one of his two air bottles ran out and he could not turn the valve on the other because his hands were so greasy. Grabbing the cable of his underwater light, he struggled towards the surface and finally managed to crack the valve. But despite their strenuous efforts it was later ascertained that there were no other survivors aboard *Truculent*.

Four years later Crabb was on board the Navy's deep-diving ship HMS *Reclaim* when her underwater television cameras identified the lost submarine HMS *Affray*, with her broken snort pipe, deep in the English Channel. It was one occasion when Crabb did not 'get m'feet wet'. The water was too deep and observation had to be made from a submerged diving chamber. When an old wartime friend, Frank Goldsworthy, a reporter on the *Daily Express*, came aboard *Reclaim*, Crabb took him below; he made much of the reunion and kept talking of the past and how he was still in the thick of diving matters. Goldsworthy wanted to go up on deck to see what was going on, but it was some time before Crabb agreed and by then all of the secret camera equipment had been covered up. This was typical of Crabb, who could abide by the rules and keep things 'hush hush' when it was required.

In 1952 Pat Rose broke off their engagement. Crabb was bitterly upset but continued with his diving, now having returned to the secrets of underwater mine warfare. Pat left England and moved to France to marry the man who was to give her the name Rose. On the rebound, Crabb met his future wife. He was married on 13 March 1952, to Mrs Margaret Elaine Player (*née* Williamson), former wife of Ernest Player.

The marriage took place at the Register Office for the district of Thanet in the County of Kent.

They lived, with her son by her previous marriage, in a caravan at West Leigh, in a field opposite the Underwater Counter Weapons Establishment (UCWE). Crabb's employment took him away on jobs and the marriage began to falter. Fellow officers of the time speak of him as being very fond of the boy, having an ability to relate to children in general. But, after one jaunt away, he returned home to find the caravan gone, along with his wife and stepson, and only his suitcase containing his personal belongings left lying in the field.

They were formally separated in April 1953. Elaine Crabb took her son to Kent, where she found employment as a typist and lived in a small cottage. Stories abounded about why the marriage failed, from the fact that Crabb was over-obsessed with diving and things of an underwater nature, to his habit of wearing a diving suit not only in the caravan but also in bed! Whatever the truth, the marriage did not last.

The same year Crabb found himself on another secret underwater job in the Canal Zone of Suez, details of which are still classified. Upon his return to England, he reported directly to the C-in-C Mediterranean, the late Earl Mountbatten of Burma, who was in England for the Coronation. Crabb had now entered the world of secret service operations.

After the dissolution of the marriage, Crabb took a single room in a tall block of service flats just beside Harrods, and this became his home whenever he worked in London. There was no telephone in the room, though the pay phone in the hall was near enough. Meals were not provided and cooking facilities consisted only of a gas ring. He hung his black frogman's suit in the wardrobe as another man might hang a golfing jacket, and settled in.

He was a sociable character who made friends easily and never lost them, and his favourite pub, the George IV, was just around the corner in Montpelier Square. He was also close to Brompton Oratory where he would meet with 'God's Butlers', as he called the priests, to whose faith he had turned during his time in Italy. By this time Pat Rose's marriage had also been dissolved, and they found themselves together again.

In August 1954 Crabb got leave of absence to spend the summer working for the Duke of Argyll, directing efforts to find gold said to be in the wreck of a Spanish galleon in Tobermory Bay, which he and Syd Knowles had tried to locate for filming purposes four years earlier. However, the venture produced no results and Crabb returned to London.

It is here that the mystery begins, for upon his arrival in London Crabb was reputed to have received a letter stating that, upon completion of his present term of service, he would not be re-entered in the Royal Navy. As a Reserve Officer he was not entitled to a pension and his service in the Royal Navy was presumed to have ended in March 1955. However, the Navy Lists of 1955 and 1956, published and printed by HMSO, enter: 'Commander (Sp.Br) L.K.P. Crabb, RNVR, GM, OBE, HMS Vernon'. This indicates that through the 1955 – 56 period, Crabb was still actually a serving officer in the Royal Navy. Officers who had served with him during and after the war recall seeing him wearing the uniform of a commander in HMS *Vernon*, during 1955. One fellow officer stands by the fact that Crabb left the Navy in 1955, and Sydney Knowles also says, that as far as he knows, Crabb left the Navy in 1955. However, Knowles agrees that he was involved with secret service type people, so could have had some connection with the Navy.

Crabb's work in Portsmouth was so secret that fellow officers would see him come and go, but did not know to whom he reported or what he actually did. He was on the Mess list of HMS *Vernon*, but would baby-sit for fellow officers rather than attend the Mess dinners, which he disliked. He had always had a dislike for formality and displayed this with an idiosyncratic variation in his uniform. At that period, naval officers had a coloured stripe between the rank stripes, depending upon their particular qualification. Crabb had pale blue between his commander's stripes and, as far as is known, no other officer used this colour for it had no official designation.

His return to 'civilian' life became centred around Maitland Pendock, a long-standing friend who owned a company called Elmbourne Ltd, which had its office in Seymour Place, London. Maitland Pendock was a London advertising consultant, a jolly middle-aged man with a round Pickwickian face. He and Crabb had been friends for over 20 years, and for the last few months Pendock had employed Crabb to sell a new type of build-it-yourself furniture, mostly to the new espresso coffee bars. Whilst in London he was not seen so often in the tweedy suits or blazer which had been his most common dress, but wore a dark business suit. He maintained a strong friendship with Pat Rose, and she recalls visiting Pendock's office on a number of occasions and getting to know him fairly well, although she did not particularly like him. On some of the visits she was introduced to other people present, and remembers meeting Anthony Blunt who was a close friend of Pendock. Burgess, Maclean and Philby were all associated with Pendock too, which suggests that the furniture business, while genuine, may also have been a front door for an MI6 clearing house. At the time, however, neither Crabb nor Pat Rose was aware of the true nature of those around them, and Pendock's son has assured us that his father had no suspicion that his friends were traitors.

Crabb's connection with Portsmouth was not over and, as Pat Rose recalls, he would often disappear for a few days and then reappear as if he had never gone. He never revealed anything about his activities other than to sometimes say he'd 'been and got m'feet wet'. Everybody knew that he'd been on an underwater job, but they never asked awkward questions. He was often seen in Portsmouth, dressed in his almost ceremonial outfit of a fawn tweed suit, a pork pie hat and his famous trademark, his sword stick. This had an over-large knob of oxidised silver and was engraved with a golden crab, designed by the person who gave him the stick, his friend Noel 'Skeffy' Fitzpatrick.

4

The Secret Service

Whatever the true role of Commander Crabb during the last months prior to his disappearance, he certainly gave the impression that he was a civilian put out of the Navy, in his words, by 'people who knew no better', and he gave those who would listen no doubt that he was not happy about it. Many of his friends were unsure of what he did, but the general view was that he worked for some government department connected with secret naval intelligence matters, for he certainly maintained contact with HMS *Vernon* in Portsmouth. Lieutenant Commander A.J.C. Dean, VRD, RNR, who had served with Crabb in Haifa, recalled: 'We next met at HMS *Vernon* in 1955 when I was on a minesweeping course, having by then become RNR. Needless to say, we had a great reunion party, but I was curious to know why he still wore wavy stripes on his uniform and lived in a caravan. I recall that he brushed it off by saying that he had been asked to stay on because of his expertise in underwater warfare. Without doubt he was the subject of curiosity by members of the Mess at *Vernon* as, although he was a Mess member, he lived apart and no one seemed to know exactly what he did or to whom he was responsible.'

In October 1955 Sydney Knowles was contacted by Crabb and asked if he would like to join him on a small job in Portsmouth. Crabb said that it would be easy and that they would get a fair fee for the job. Knowles accepted and met Crabb in London, where he was introduced to Matthew Smith. Smith was an American with the CIA, who were organising a mission to look under the soviet cruiser *Sverdlov*. The cruiser had displayed a good turn of speed on entering Portsmouth very quickly, and seemed to be very manoeuvrable. The British and Americans both wanted to know what made the vessel so versatile. Because the ship was in British waters, it had to be an outside job, so it was organised under the CIA umbrella.

Crabb and Knowles had diving equipment from their wartime exploits, which was of Italian origin. They travelled to Portsmouth with Smith and, during the hours of darkness, dressed in two-piece diving suits, donned their breathing sets and entered the water. On their heads they had skull caps with black veils. The latter was netting which hung down over the head and face, which allowed them to see but broke up the silhouettes of their heads when on the surface. They reached the stern of the cruiser and dived down to the propellers and rudder, finding nothing out of place or unusual. They then moved to the bilge keel, where a signal informed Knowles to remain where he was whilst Crabb went forward. After about ten minutes Crabb returned and signalled for Knowles to follow him forward. The two men moved to the bow, where Knowles found himself on the edge of a large circular opening in the bottom of the hull.

Knowles waited on the edge whilst Crabb went up inside where he examined a propeller. It was evident that the propeller could be lowered and directed to give thrust to the bow and aid the ship's manoeuvring. After the inspection both men moved away from the ship to swim back to their rendezvous and report to Smith. They changed into dry civilian clothes and Crabb returned to London while Knowles returned home.

The cruiser *Sverdlov* was on a visit to take part in the Spithead review and was anchored at sea in clear water. It is said that whilst the ship was at anchor a naval clearance diving team was dropped off to move with the current on a covert underwater survey of the hull. They used closed circuit breathing apparatus so as to remain undetected, and were picked up well clear of the cruiser. It is 'said' that they found nothing worth reporting. This operation is believed to have been a separate operation from the one carried out by Crabb and Knowles, and could well have been undertaken to confirm Crabb's findings and obtain more details.

It was known that the Soviet authorities were aware of Crabb's exploits under the cruiser, and corroborated evidence later provided by Anatoli Golitsin, a Soviet defector, revealed that Crabb had been placed high on the list of wanted people. He was a most experienced and knowledgeable expert on almost every type of underwater mine and explosive, and indeed underwater warfare in general. With the formation of the Soviet *Spetsnaz* special swimmer brigades it is evident that anybody with Crabb's experience would be of untold value. The Soviet source stated that it had been decided that Commander Crabb should be taken into the Soviet Union as soon as it was feasible.

However, they knew that Crabb was loyal to Queen and Country and could not be enticed to defect. In fact, his loyalty often went to extremes. He was a converted Roman Catholic and as such followed the Church's line and abhorred the Soviet system. To 'capture' Commander Crabb they were going to have to have a foolproof plan, preferably one which got him over at the request of his own people.

The Soviet secret service would have known a great deal about Crabb for, whatever his connections were with Pendock, it was possible that Pendock's business was a clearing house for MI6. Soviet agents had already established themselves in the British secret service, as was to be revealed with some embarrassment to the government over the years to come. The double agents would have known about Crabb and his covert underwater operations and may have at some stage been involved with them. From this inside operation Soviet intelligence would have been aware that both the British and Americans were desperate to obtain details of the Soviet secret swimmer units, but whether the Soviets sowed the seeds or whether the British played unwittingly into their hands can only be guessed at. Certainly, the events that followed the Crabb incident showed that it was a far more important expedition than a mere look at the hull of a cruiser. British intelligence wanted to know about the secret swimmer units in the Soviet Union, whilst the Russians for their part wanted Crabb.

Could British and US intelligence infiltrate an agent into the Soviet Union, somebody who knew a lot about diving? That person would have to be acceptable to the Russians, for anybody guilty of espionage would certainly be executed. They needed someone whom the Russians would accept into the fold, especially if they thought he could help them. Once the man was in he could, after a period of time, join the Red Navy; he would then have access to the swimmer units, details of which, through British and American contacts, he could pass back. When he had gathered as much useful intelligence data as possible, they could get him out. The plan was bold and involved a lot of risk, but even if it did go wrong the agent would be disowned. That was all part of being a member of the service.

Crabb fitted the bill on every aspect. He was already used by naval intelligence and was familiar with covert operations. He had the knowledge and experience the Russians would be keen to have, for he was already high on their list of wanted men. They would not kill him but would prefer to use him, especially if he agreed to join them. He was the right age, in Soviet thinking, for they place great store on the authority of the older man. Furthermore, Crabb had no close family ties, and above all he was desperate to accept any diving job. If he were not seen for a while everybody would say, 'It's old Crabbie, up to his tricks again,' and shrug off any further suspicions.

The intelligence service had been warned in 1956 by the Prime Minister, Sir Anthony Eden, not to undertake any covert intelligence operations against Soviet visitors or their ships during their stay in Portsmouth. This operation was different and, so as to avoid risking its cancellation, it was never taken to higher authorities. Thus, when they said that they were unaware of any diving operations against the Soviet ships, they were telling the truth. To maintain the operation out of the British sphere, the CIA were brought in to control it as they had the year before. Matthew Smith was again directed to control the operation and Commander Crabb would have been presented with the plan and asked to undertake the mission.

Crabb would never have had a second thought: he would have been delighted to be given the opportunity to serve Queen and Country again. His number two from the Italian days, the American naval officer Tony Marsloe, was also involved, although no details of his status are available. Crabb would have been briefed to talk about doing another 'bottom' job in Portsmouth to provoke the Russians into action. It is certain that the Russians were keeping an eye on Crabb and it seems equally certain that a serious leak could derive from Pendock's business. Once the Russians knew that Crabb was to go under the ship, they would be prepared to make the capture. To facilitate this, he was to make the dive in daylight and show himself near the ships.

Once taken to Russia he would be subjected to Soviet interrogation, and he would have to impart a certain amount of information. However, he had been away from the mines section long enough not to have recent knowledge. If he were offered a place in the Soviet Navy, he should accept to win their confidence and gather information. Once the intelligence agencies had all the information they needed, or if they felt it otherwise necessary, they would get him out. Of course, if anything went wrong, then Crabb was on his own. Because of the political situation, the CIA moved in Matthew Smith as the controller and he undertook certain actions that were both to establish a great deal of mystery and link the job with outside organisations. This in effect is what happened when things went wrong, for the planners were unaware of the Soviet agents' infiltration and knowledge of their intentions.

Crabb needed an assistant so he telephoned Knowles and told him that a very important job had been proposed – he could not discuss it – but he wanted Knowles to come along with him. Knowles reluctantly turned the job down. For his part, he would have followed Crabb anywhere out of pure loyalty to the man, but personal problems at home dictated his decision to say no. When Crabb insisted that it was very important and involved their old friend Tony Marsloe from the Italian days, Knowles linked the American with the CIA and wondered what was so important under the new ship's hull, as they had reported her sister ship less than a year previously. He had to decline Crabb's offer.

Pat Rose, who was introduced to Matthew Smith by Crabb, recalls: 'Crabb really liked Smith, I did not – there was something about him – I can't explain what. I remember that he was always cracking jokes. He was tall, in his late thirties, with dark hair and a moustache.' She pondered a moment. 'He was always well dressed on the three occasions that I met him but above all, and most important, he was an American.' The fact that he was American was queried. 'Yes, he was an American.' That fact was corroborated by Nag's Head landlord Len Cole, who had also been introduced to him by Crabb, and by Syd Knowles who had worked with him on the *Sverdlov* job.

Pat Rose told us that after Smith had gone she asked Crabb what he was doing with an American who was 'not a very nice person'. Crabb said that he was all right and would not discuss the matter any further.

Each time Pat Rose met him she disliked him more, but for Crabb the reverse applied.

To ensure that the Russians were made aware of the forthcoming dive, Crabb made it known that he was going to do a 'little job' in Portsmouth which involved getting his feet wet. He was totally unaware that the Russians already knew of the plan and would be prepared for him.

Crabb made Pendock aware of his impending visit to Portsmouth, and only when we were talking to her did Pat Rose see the possible implications of the leak of Crabb's 'job' coming from there. 'That man Blunt was a close friend of Pendock's and neither I nor Crabbie would have connected the possible implications.'

To the housekeeper at the service flat in Hans Road where he lived, Crabb made no secret of the fact that he had been called upon to do another job for the Admiralty. Len Cole was also told when Crabb engaged him in conversation at the Nag's Head public house.

Crabb hated letter-writing, and even Pat Rose confirmed that he never wrote to her even when he was away. Before he departed from London for the visit to Portsmouth, however, he wrote to Petty Officer David Bell (a member of the Gibraltar team, though no relation to the original Leading Seaman Bell) saying how pleased he had been to meet up with him again. Crabb even wrote to the publishers of the forthcoming book which Marshall Pugh was writing, a rare occurrence indeed for they had difficulty in getting him to make vital alterations to the manuscript. He also wrote to his mother and told her that he was going on a special job but not to worry for he would be all right. He instructed her to tear the letter up after she had read it – she told friends that was not like her Lionel and she was worried.

It was apparent to Crabb's friends that he was concerned about the job ahead, and that he had not been sleeping well. Pat Rose found him awkward and not himself. She asked him 'Why are you like this?' He replied that he did not know. He asked her to marry him. She told him that she could not marry him just like that, she would need time to think about it, and anyway he was not behaving normally. He then asked if they could become engaged again and she agreed, but he told her that she would have to wait for the ring until he had 'done a job' in Portsmouth.

Crabb telephoned Knowles again to see whether he had changed his mind – Knowles told him that he had not. Crabb went on to say that he could not use any of the divers from HMS *Vernon* as they could not be implicated if things went wrong and so he would have to go it alone. Knowles told him, as a friend, to call the job off, but Crabb replied that he could not for it was most important. That was the last time Knowles spoke to Crabb.

Marshall Pugh relates that a meeting to finalise details for the Portsmouth job was made at Pendock's business, when Smith bought two tables for £4 18s 0d (£4.90). The sectioned tables were to be taken away in a private car, and because the buyer was a friend of Crabb a cheque was accepted. It was signed by Bernard★ Smith and drawn on the South Kensington branch of Lloyds Bank, but it was dated 1955 instead of 1956. Crabb said to Pendock, 'All right, give me the cheque. I shall be seeing him when I go to Portsmouth.'

On Tuesday 17 April 1956, Crabb met Pat for a drink, but he was obviously on edge and chain-smoked his cigarettes. He sipped his drink, which Pat said was most unusual; it was certainly 'not her normal Crabbie'. They had always been close to each other during any crisis in their lives and helped each other. She asked him what was wrong. He shrugged the question off and to change the subject decided that they should go to Len's for lunch.

At the Nag's Head he remained quiet and they ordered a meal. Crabbie was still in a strange mood, Pat recalled, and Len was aware of it. Out of the blue Crabb asked Pat: 'Will you come down to Portsmouth with me?'

'But, Crabbie, why?' Pat responded.

'I'd like you to,' he said.

'Good gracious, Crabbie, you want me to come all the way to Portsmouth and go back again!' She paused, then pleaded; 'Why, Crabbie, why?'

He looked at her and then said quietly, 'I want you to come but you will have to come back on your own as I am staying down there.'

She returned his look and frowned. 'No Crabbie, I'm not going all

★Despite the Christian name on the cheque, Pat Rose was and Syd Knowles is convinced that Bernard and Matthew Smith were one and the same person. As an American intelligence agent he would, in any case, have used different names for different purposes wherever possible.

that way for no reason, you've been alone before when you've been on one of your jaunts so why do you want me to go now – no, Crabbie, I'm not coming.'

Len Cole heard that part of the conversation and interrupted: 'That's a bit mean, Pat, you should go down.' She again refused but something in Len's voice made her change her mind and she agreed to accompany Crabb.

They boarded the Portsmouth train at Victoria Station and found an empty compartment. Crabb moved to a corner seat and stared out of the window. For the most part he almost ignored Pat and seemed deep in thought. As the journey progressed Pat could stand it no longer, and again she asked him what was wrong. He relented enough to tell her that he was going to try out some new and secret underwater equipment. She laughed as she told him that he had tried out all sorts of equipment before and that he had been excited – not in this strange mood. Her request for details drew a blank as Crabb evaded any further questions, until she told him that if he did not come clean she would call off the engagement. She was at the end of her tether over this strange mood of his.

Crabb relented and told her that he was going to look at the bottom of a Russian cruiser. Pat was taken aback and demanded to know why, as he'd been under the other ship only months before. His only reply was that it was for his Queen and Country and that they came even before her. He told her that he loved her and always had but he had a special job to do.

'But you're mad,' was her response. She asked how he thought that he would get away with it, for the Russians would guard the ship day and night. He avoided her eyes before telling her that he and Syd had looked at the *Sverdlov* before and had encountered no problems. She demanded to know if Syd was going to dive. Crabb replied that he was not. She then pleaded with him not to do the job and to return to London with her. He told her that he was committed.

In a quiet voice, she asked who was sending him on such a risky job. He replied that it was the Admiralty. She did not believe him and he conceded that it was only indirectly connected with the Admiralty. This made her angry and she asked who else was involved. He told her that it was a very important job and that it was top secret. Because of that, the Admiralty could not be seen to be involved. They sat in silence while he smoked. He took out his wallet and removed the photographs that he had of her, one taken in the south of France with her brother and sister-in-law and one of her sitting beside a swimming pool. He obviously treasured them, and after having looked at them for a while he returned them to his wallet. Then they sat in silence.

When Crabb next spoke it was to tell Pat that he would be back in London the next day but that, if anything went wrong and he could not dive, it would be the following day. However, he asked her not to worry as everything would be all right as it was 'all being arranged'.*

Pat did not accept this and asked who was organising the job. Quietly, he told her that it was Matthew Smith. In a high voice she asked what Smith had to do with an Admiralty job and repeated that she did not trust him. She asked again why he was not dealing with British naval officers as he always had.

Crabb tried to explain that Smith was an American intelligence officer and that, because of possible repercussions from a British organised job, it was to be done outside the usual channels. It was not, he said, a normal job. Pat shook her head and told him that it was not right and to call it off. His final words were that he had to do the job for his Queen and Country and that there was no going back.

When they arrived at Portsmouth, she told him that he could take her to the Queens Hotel for tea and that it might 'cheer him up'. He told her quietly that he was not staying at the Queens; Matthew Smith was arranging things and he had to meet him now. She showed her anger by referring to Smith as that 'terrible American'. Crabb defended him. They waited at the station for the train to depart for London. It was an uneasy time for Pat as she knew something lay heavily on Crabb's mind. He took her into an empty compartment where they said their goodbyes and she watched him walk through the barrier, to disappear from her life.

---

*With the advantage of the evidence to follow, the words 'all being arranged' take on a double meaning. Crabb *knew* he would not be back within the next couple of days. His reticence throughout the day towards his fiancée was caused by the discomfort of lying to her.

5

The Portsmouth Operation

A black saloon car brought the next stage of the Crabb mystery to the cobbled High Street of Portsmouth on the evening of Tuesday 17 April 1956 – Budget Day. The car ran slowly along the filled-up tram lines and pulled in past the Sally Port Hotel. A waitress preparing dinner tables in the bow-windowed dining room saw two men get out.

The Sally Port Hotel, a four-storeyed 200-year-old building, is double fronted and was painted in cream and blue with gilt lettering. It is the centre of the old town of Portsmouth, famous in Britain's naval history, by the ancient and historic Sally Port from which Admiral Horatio Nelson sailed and beside which Admiral Anson lived. Fifty yards from the hotel door was a metal plaque greened with salt spume which read: 'NEAR THIS PLACE NAVAL HEROES INNUMERABLE HAVE EMBARKED TO FIGHT THEIR COUNTRY'S BATTLES . . .'

The two men entered and approached the hotelier, 53-year-old Mr Edward Richman, who, in white coat, was seated in the square-paned reception and was very busy. It was about 8 pm, the twenty-room hotel was full except for two top rooms, numbers 17 and 20. Most of the guests were businessmen connected with shipbuilding, and a couple were Admiralty inspectors.

When one of the two men asked about accommodation Mr Richman told them: 'There are two attic rooms. I am sorry I cannot show you them at the moment, but here are the keys. Be good chaps and have a look at them if you like . . .'

The keys were handed to the taller of the two men. He was casually dressed in a lightweight suit, and was about 37-years-old. This is the man who signed the register as Smith. He took the smaller of the two rooms – number 17, a single – to allow his companion, Lionel Crabb, to take the larger, more comfortable number 20. Lionel Crabb was casually dressed, wearing a greenish tweed suit with brown shoes and green woven tie. His only luggage was a briefcase.

Crabb's room had two dry-oak beams, like ship's timbers, bracing the dormer roof. The square window overlooked Vosper's shipyard, part of the dockyard and harbour. In the centre of the view was the South Railway jetty – the berth to be occupied by the Russian cruiser carrying Bulganin and Khrushchev on a 'goodwill' visit, framed with a forest of cranes and masts, with stretches of harbour water with ferry boats, sails and smoke.

Witnesses detailed the movements of both Crabb and his companion Smith.

Tuesday 17 April. Time: 8 pm. Both arrived at the Sally Port Hotel. Neither took dinner. Crabb appeared in the Porthole Bar of the Sally Port at about 8.30. He drank two whiskies.

Time: 9 pm. Crabb went out. He returned at 9.30 expecting to see Smith in the bar. 'I'll go up to see if my friend would like a drink,' he said.

Time: 9.45 pm. Crabb returned alone, smiled and said: 'He has gone to bed.'

When asked about morning tea Crabb replied: 'I shall be out early, so don't bother about a call, tea, or papers. Don't bother with number 17 either. We shall both be out early.' He accepted from Mr Richman front door Yale keys for himself and Smith, 'in case we might be out late'. So, after a nightcap of whisky and water, Commander Crabb left the bar, presumably for bed, at 10.30. Nobody remembers seeing him again that night.

Wednesday 18 April: The brass barometer in the Sally Port Hotel was set at Fair, and it was a mild spring morning. The hotel life awoke at about 7 am, but nobody saw either Crabb or Smith. They were out early.

High tides for this day were at 4.32 am and 5.26 pm.

Time: about 8.30 Crabb walked into the hotel, had eggs and bacon for breakfast and read a newspaper.

Time: 9.30 am. He looked out through the net curtains up and down the High Street as if expecting somebody. Suddenly he rose and walked out.

Sightseers crowded around the dock area of Portsmouth to watch the arrival of the Soviet warships. The principal ship, the cruiser *Ordzhonikidze*, moved into the harbour faster than would normally be expected from a ship of her size, as had her sister ship *Sverdlov* before, and displayed the ability to stop and manoeuvre rapidly over a short distance. Following the cruisers were two destroyers, the *Smotryaschci* and the *Sovershenny*. The *Ordzhonikidze* moved alongside at the South Railway jetty at Portsmouth Royal Naval Dockyard. Her bows faced up-river, with stern towards the sea. The two Soviet destroyers moved alongside the cruiser and moored. Interest in the ships was twofold: first, they were part of the 'new' Soviet Navy and second, and probably of more interest, was the fact that the cruiser carried Mr Khrushchev and Mr Bulganin.

The *Sverdlov* Class cruisers were considered to be large and fast, displacing some 19,200 tons, and having a maximum speed of 34.5 knots. Their overall length of 689 feet (207 metres) and a beam of 70 feet (21 metres) served as a platform for a considerable array of weapons. The main armament comprised twelve six-inch (152.4-mm) guns, mounted in four triple turrets. Secondary armament was in the form of twelve 3.9-inch (101.6-mm) guns, mounted in six twin mounts. Anti-aircraft firepower came from thirty-two 37-mm guns. As with current ship design at that period, additional weapons consisted of 21-inch (533.4-mm) torpedo tubes and between 140 and 240 mines. The complement was some 1,050 officers and men.

Commander Crabb would have observed the ships entering the harbour and berthing in the dockyard confines. The shape and size of the cruiser would have been familiar to him from his exploration of the *Sverdlov* the year before.

Crabb returned to the hotel at about 7 pm, where he made a telephone call. He proceeded to the bar and had a drink and then went in to dinner. When he had finished dinner he left the hotel, and walked towards Portsmouth centre and the railway station.

Before 9 o'clock he was in Havant, at the Bear's Head Hotel, where he met an old friend, Lieutenant Commander John Crawford, RN, and his dark-haired wife Daphne. This encounter had been arranged by telephone beforehand.

Petty Officer 'Lofty' Gordon – he is six feet four inches tall and weighs fourteen and a half stone – was drinking in the Bear's Head by 'coincidence' when Commander Crabb walked in with the Crawfords. Gordon, a Naval diver, was a friend of all three. He moved across to greet Crabb, and it appeared to the Crawfords that he had not seen him for several months.

Daphne Crawford, recalling their meeting, said: 'It was grand to see Crabbie again. He sometimes called to see us on his occasional visits to Portsmouth. This evening we were at the Bear's Head Hotel and chatted fairly generally over a drink or two. I can remember no mention of frogmen or diving. We talked about a furniture business in which Commander Crabb was interested. We did not leave the Bear until about 10 o'clock, when we dropped him off the taxi at Havant railway station, for his return to Portsmouth.'

When Crabb left to go back to Havant station with the Crawfords, 'Lofty' Gordon shook hands with him and said: 'Good luck'. Gordon did not return to Portsmouth with Crabb.

Nobody saw or heard Crabb return to the Sally Port Hotel that night; nobody had seen Smith go or return. So the last friends to have seen Crabb before his 'disappearance' were the Crawfords, on the night of 18 April.

By 7 am the following morning, the time of the earliest staff activity at the Sally Port Hotel, Crabb had already let himself out of the front door. Smith must also have left early, for not one of the staff caught sight of him either. High tide was at 5.54 am and 6.53 pm.

Breakfast was laid for Crabb at a single table near the window. The waitress ticked off the guests at breakfast by the numbers of their rooms. When she cleared the tables only two numbers were left . . . 17 and 20.

Crabb, number 20, never came back.

It was mid-morning, round about 11.30, when Mr Smith appeared at the reception desk alone. He asked for both bills. 'We are leaving today,' he said. The total bill for two nights' bed and breakfast, and one extra dinner, was £3 16s (£3.80), which was paid in cash. Then Mr Smith hurried out, carrying two bags.

Smith departed from Portsmouth, having removed Crabb's belongings from the room and taken them with him. The Admiralty later returned Crabb's clothes to his mother, but Smith's cheque from the London meeting and the photographs he had looked at on the train with Pat Rose were not with them. The swordstick, Crabb's talisman, was also missing, and all investigations by the media or Crabb's family to find it drew blanks. Nobody knew at that time where it was.

In his book *Commander Crabb is Alive*, Bernard Hutton gives a rather vivid account of events and conversations between Crabb and Smith. This must be put down to pure conjecture for unless he discussed it with either man it can only be poetic licence and there is no known meeting between Hutton and Smith. Having said that, we have verified through our own sources that many of the points and events did take place.

Crabb had been assigned the 'job' and now entered HMS *Vernon*, the Navy's diving centre. This aroused no alarm, for he was 'on the books' and was often seen in and around the base, which he had often termed his second home. He would without doubt have been greeted by fellow officers who, because of his past exploits and status at the base, would have connected his appearance with that of the visiting Russian ships.

Once in the base Crabb went to the diving store where he met the duty petty officer, who knew him. When, as was widely reported, however, he made a request for oxygen, he was turned down and told that he could not be supplied with any owing to the forthcoming visit. The petty officer then excused himself and departed to get a meal . . . leaving Crabb alone.

Our information is that, at that time, there were two diving stores, one for clearance divers, which housed all of their equipment, and another for the standard diving equipment. Our informant told us that the person in charge of the standard diving store was Petty Officer 'Lofty' Gordon, whom Crabb knew very well and had, of course, met only the night before. It is presumed that Crabb's visit was to the standard diving store where his special closed-circuit equipment was stored, as he remained apart from the normal diving operations of *Vernon*.

His equipment was of Italian manufacture, unique to Crabb, and was part of his obsession for everything Italian. One of the major differences between this equipment and RN issue is the screw fittings from the bottle to the apparatus: the thread is different, so British bottles would not fit Crabb's equipment. He would have needed to fill his bottle separately, using special connections; he certainly could not have just entered a store and helped himself. The visit to the store must have been official. He would have checked his equipment which was stored in a wicker basket, and it was not the sort of thing he could carry out of the gate without anybody seeing him. One thing is certain, and that is that, with a strict clampdown on any form of spying or covert operations during the visit, Crabb would not − if he were not on official business − have been allowed near the diving store, or for that matter near HMS *Vernon* itself.

If, as stated by many different sources, Crabb was in HMS *Vernon*, it is probable that he was taken with his diving equipment to Horsea Island, where the Navy has a training lake. Here he could have undertaken distance swims and practised his underwater navigation, as indicated by a telephone call made to Pendock when Crabb told him that everything was all right and said that he was in better shape than he thought. Having made the dive his equipment would be prepared for the operation.

Once the equipment was checked he would, if he had not already done so, have reported to somebody who would have advised him of the tide status and weather conditions for the coming days. He would have been given a report on vessel movements and any other operations in the Portsmouth area that could have affected the job. Finally, he would have been provided with details of the entry point, and the passes needed to get him and Smith there, so as not to arouse any interest.

There is evidence that some officers who knew Crabb connected his presence with the impending visit; they saw Crabb going into a perilous situation, and warned him about the Soviet security precautions. During the day lookouts were posted, scouring the waters around the ships, whilst at night powerful floodlights played on the water, and more lookouts searched for any trace of an underwater operation.

Crabb was breaking every rule for a covert underwater operation, for these are generally done at night when, if the divers encounter any trouble, they can surface and use the cover of darkness to try to get away unseen. This job was to be done in daylight, when any need to break the surface would be spotted. That, in this instance, was exactly what Crabb required.

It is apparent that Crabb and Smith let themselves out of the Sally Port Hotel before 7 am on 19 April. They used the car, which was driven by Smith the short distance past HMS *Vernon* to the main naval dockyard. Stopping at the guardroom they showed their passes, which had been provided during Crabb's briefing, and were waved past, allowing them access to the dockyard area. Inside, they drove to the pre-determined spot where the operation was to begin.

As the dive was undertaken from within the dockyard a number of locations and options were available. One was the boat pound situated to the right of the road that leads from the main gate to HMS *Victory*; this area is used for storing small boats and lies below the old sail or rigging store. Access to and from the pound is through a tunnel which runs under the road and buildings until it reaches the harbour waters. This option would have given cover to the divers for entry, and they could have travelled to the entrance by boat, for the opening was close to the berth of the cruiser.

The other option available and favoured by most investigators into the subject was to use the Kings Stairs (steps). This area was again hidden from the view of the Russian ships, and was also an area frequently used by divers at that period for access into the harbour. Again it was close to the Russian ships, and they could, by using either of these entry points, have followed the dock wall whilst underwater.

I have been told that Crabb was supported by a small team of naval divers, no more than four in number. The team was to escort Crabb to the vicinity of the Russian ships, then allow him to go his own way; they were to return to the start point, and were under orders not to compromise their position or take any risk that would cause them to be 'captured'. They did not know what the plan was, or what Crabb was to do.

The naval diving team arrived in a covered truck and met up with Crabb and Smith. Having arrived dressed in their rubber dry suits, they waited whilst Crabb dressed in his. There has been much confusion about the different types of suits used, and Crabb's was totally different from those worn by the naval divers.

The standard naval issue dry suit of that period consisted of a one-piece flexible rubber suit with built-in reinforced feet. The sleeves had thin rubber cuffs which sealed against the diver's wrists. Entry into the suit was through the neck, so the neck area was made of a very strong elastic rubber, which enabled it to be pulled open. At the neck the rubber fitted onto a metal ring, which kept it away from the neck and lifted it clear of the diver's shoulders. A hood of thin flexible rubber covered the diver's head and fitted onto the ring, where a clamp held suit and hood in place, while the hood itself fitted closely round the head, making a watertight seal at both the face and the neck. A diver in thick undergarments should, providing the suit had no leaks, keep warm and dry.

The Pirelli or Heinke dry suit which Crabb wore differed in a number of ways from the naval issue. This suit was a two-piece flexible rubber garment, with the lower part having built-in reinforced feet. The top part of the suit overlapped the bottom and was loose-fitting. This allowed the two parts to be folded together to make a joint. A rubber band was put on to cover the joint, to hold the two parts together and ensure a watertight seal. This suit also had a rubber seal at the wrists, but the neck did not require a separate seal, for a thin flexible rubber collar fitted against the neck, making it also watertight. This suit could be worn with or without a hood. If a hood was worn it would be loose-fitting and used for protection and insulation.

The breathing equipment used by Crabb and the naval divers also differed. The Royal Navy's Underwater Breathing Apparatus (UBA) is a relatively small and compact set that uses the closed-circuit principle: the breathing gas is recycled within the system, rather than the expired gas being discharged into the water, as is the case with compressed air diving equipment. Combat swimmers use this system because it is compact and gives off no tell-tale bubbles to give them away. It has one disadvantage in that it uses pure oxygen, which restricts the operational depth to ten metres (33 feet). This is because oxygen becomes toxic when used below this depth. There is a built-in safety margin but this is only broken under extreme emergencies.

The UBA comprises a vest which fits over the head to rest on the shoulders. At the front, in line with the chest, is a flexible bag, the counter lung. In the centre of the bag is a round canister containing protosorb. Soda-lime granules absorb the carbon dioxide produced when the diver breathes out. A flexible concertina hose connects the protosorb canister to the bottom of the full face mask, and has, on the inside, a mouthpiece through which the diver breathes. The face mask has a round glass face plate inserted into a soft rubber moulding which fits the full extent of the face, sealing onto the rubber hood. It is held in place by adjustable rubber straps.

The counter lung is supplied with oxygen from a small oxygen bottle set under the bag; the diver opens and closes the bottle to fill it. If the bag should be overfilled, a relief valve discharges masses of minute bubbles, ideally disperse and do not show on the surface. When the bag is breathed down, it is refilled the same way.

To balance the diver when in the water, ball weights are carried in a small pouch on the upper part of the back of the vest. These can be released by the diver in an emergency. Because of this method of ballasting, the diver does not require a weight belt.

The Italian system worked on the same principle. It differed in so far as it was smaller and more compact than the Royal Navy's and was a firm favourite with Commander Crabb who had used it in Italy. No full face mask was worn, only a small half mask similar to those in use today by SCUBA divers. It did not have any built-in weight system, so when wearing a dry suit the diver had to wear a separate weight belt. The breathing tube travelled from the protosorb canister directly to the mouthpiece, which meant that it fitted directly into the diver's mouth.

The Royal Navy greatly preferred their own system, reasoning, that, if a diver passed out whilst underwater, the mouthpiece of the UBA would remain in his mouth, and the mask would prevent drowning. The fact that the mouthpiece could not be accidentally knocked out of the diver's mouth was also a safeguard when moving about in black water conditions. With the Italian system it was also possible for small amounts of water to seep past the mouth and down the hose to mix with the protosorb, causing a 'cocktail' that was harmful to the diver – hence its nickname, 'one breath from death'. However, Crabb had used the Italian system in every conceivable situation and would hear nothing said against it.

When Crabb and the Naval divers were dressed and ready to enter the water, the final words of the briefing would have been given to ensure that each man knew what he had to do. Standing in the water with fins (flippers) on his feet, each man opened his oxygen bottle to allow the gas to enter and fill the counter lung. They then drew long, deep breaths, drawing the oxygen through the protosorb, up into their lungs and then expired out through the same hose into the canister which removed the carbon dioxide, before the gas re-entered the bag. This was done until the bag was almost empty, when it refilled and the process repeated, the idea being to remove any dangerous gases and ensure that the system was working. On the third charge, the divers were ready to enter the water. It had taken only two minutes to prepare the breathing sets.

Entry into the water would have been done quietly, each man submerging up to his shoulders. The air trapped inside the suit goes to the highest point and to vent it out the diver raises both arms and pulls the cuffs away from his wrists, allowing the air to escape. This also helps to adjust each man's buoyancy. The divers would then have submerged, breathing on the apparatus, allowing the person on the surface to look for any tell-tale bubbles from a leak. With everything checked out as being in good order, the man on the surface would have signalled with a thumbs-up. Returning the signal, the divers disappeared below the surface, connected by rope in pairs.

Breathing in and out in a steady rhythm, the divers moved off on their journey to the cruiser *Ordzhonikidze*. The *Ordzhonikidze* had a maximum draught of 26 feet (7.9 m) which was well within the operational capabilities of the apparatus. Their task would have been made easier by the fact that they could follow the dock wall, leading them straight to the target. The water would have been murky with very little visibility.

The diver who was buddied with Crabb (connected by a short rope) was released from him close to the ship. The naval divers then watched as Crabb disappeared from sight, having given the thumbs-up, into the murky gloom of Portsmouth harbour waters. Whilst Crabb found the cruiser and prepared to swim to a location where he would surface, the naval divers began their swim back to the point of entry where they reported to Smith that Crabb had been 'delivered'. In the meantime, Crabb had surfaced, been spotted and captured.

The naval divers remained dressed in their diving equipment and boarded the covered transport. They returned to their base, whilst Matthew Smith reported for a debrief before returning to the Sally Port Hotel. Smith's part of the operation was completed. Crabb had been planted aboard the Russian cruiser.

There were no special anti-diver clamps or other devices awaiting him; Crabb simply surfaced, remained long enough to ensure that he was seen, whereupon the Russian divers went into action, and after a skirmish took him to the cruiser. If Crabb really had been looking under the cruiser, and had an equipment failure, he would have surfaced close to the hull, which would have afforded him some shelter from observation; he would then have to have ditched his weight belt and breathing set and made a swim of it. But contemporary newspaper reports state that he remained on the surface face up. If he needed to clear the set, as he had done at the beginning of the dive, he would have done it out of sight, and there were suitable places amid the mooring pontoons where he could have done so.

He is then said to have gone below the surface again, where the Russians would have had no hope of finding him if he did not want to be found. As Syd Knowles pointed out, 'Look how many hours police divers spend searching for a body in a pond, and we are talking about the vast expanse of Portsmouth harbour'.

And what of Soviet Security? The best defence against any form of underwater investigation would have been to have the ship's ASDIC operating. Sonar emits a sound wave that would drastically affect a diver, and he would have to abort his dive. It is still the most effective measure used today, apart from turning the screws, which in the *Ordzhonikidze*'s case would have been impractical with three ships berthed together.

During their stay, the Soviet ships would have been under constant observation by naval personnel at HMS *Vernon* and other establishments, who would have maintained a log of events. All naval diving teams were put on alert for the period of the visit, although they did not undertake any operations. Contrary to the Admiralty reports there were no experiments at Stokes Bay. It is reported by one source that a naval diving team was moved to a new location during the period of the Crabb dive. Questioned about the reasons for such a move, it was said that the team had to be officially 'unaware' of the operation, so that they could not be connected with it if problems arose.

The naval watch on the morning of 18 April is said to have comprised a lieutenant and a petty officer, who are claimed by Bernard Hutton to have witnessed and recorded the following course of events. They observed Russian divers enter the water and remain near the cruiser. They then saw another diver on the surface, alone, between the cruiser and one of the destroyers. They watched the Russian divers move towards the lone diver. There was a skirmish and all of the divers disappeared under the water near the cruiser. This action is said to have taken place at the stern of the ships, whilst other reports place the incident off the bows, out of view of the *Vernon* observers. The naval watch continued to observe the Russian vessels but saw nothing more of the divers. Details of the events were recorded in the duty log book and all of the information was passed immediately to the Admiralty and other government departments in London.

Other witnesses came forward and made statements about the incident. Former Petty Officer Peter Fleetway who was aboard HMS *Starling*, moored barely 100 yards away from the *Ordzhonikidze* on the morning of Crabb's dive, recalls that 'I was struck by the unusual activity going on around the cruiser'. The last thing Fleetway saw was 'three frogmen suddenly surface. They made for one of the small boats. Two of the trio pushed the other into it. The other frogmen clustered round. The boat headed for the climbing ladder.'

Another reliable source stated that all personnel at HMS *Vernon* in any way connected with the 'event' were, before the Crabb story made the newspapers, given overseas postings, so that when the press arrived in Portsmouth those who knew anything were out of the United Kingdom. All officers who knew Crabb and were aware that he had been in Portsmouth were quizzed by the authorities to find out if he had said anything about what he was up to. They were then told to speak about the matter to no one.

6

The Cover-Up

The Admiralty never announced the disappearance of Commander Crabb to the world; they only admitted it ten days later when the first newspaper enquiry was received. In those ten days, a private drama was played out between the Admiralty and Crabb's relatives and friends, which has probably never had its equal in peacetime.

Maitland Pendock was a little worried when he had not heard from Crabb by Thursday night and he became quite anxious when Friday passed without Crabb returning. On Saturday Pendock telephoned the Sally Port Hotel to enquire after Crabb, and was told that he had left on Thursday. Knowing that Crabb had many friends and colleagues in HMS *Vernon* and the Portsmouth area, he then phoned the navy base. The duty officer at the gate stated that he had not seen Commander Crabb and told Pendock to hold while he made enquiries. These drew a blank as he had not been seen in the wardroom or by any of the officers in the Portsmouth area.

That Saturday evening, casting around for possible explanations, Pendock phoned Commander Crawford. Crawford and his wife Daphne had not seen Crabb since Wednesday night, and said that he had failed to keep a date with them on Friday evening. Pendock explained that he had no knowledge of Crabb's whereabouts. Now Commander Crawford was worried and he told Pendock that he would make enquiries at HMS *Vernon*. It was arranged that Pendock should call back the next day. Pendock phoned on the Sunday and Crawford explained that he had not been able to discover anything and said that he was going to the Admiralty to try and sort things out.

It seemed significant that Crawford never reported the result of his enquiries at the Admiralty and that he was not available during the next few days.

Pat Rose was also desperately worried. She phoned Pendock and told him she was afraid that the Russians had captured him, but Pendock gave no indication that he was concerned. He said that Crabb would be behind a mermaid or a rock and laughed it off.

On the morning of Saturday 21 April 1956, Detective Superintendent Stanley Lamport, chief of Portsmouth CID, called at the Sally Port Hotel and spoke to Edward Richman. He asked to look at the hotel register. It was passed to him and he began looking through it. He then removed four pages, neatly and with care. These pages covered the first weeks in April 1956. Mr Richman raised an objection and said that hotel registers must not, according to the regulations, be tampered with. Superintendent Lamport told him that he was acting on orders from a much higher authority. He signed the next page as a form of receipt, to satisfy the proprietor. Before leaving, the police officer told Richman that the matter was very serious and that he should tell his staff not to talk to anybody about it, especially the press, as it was covered by the Official Secrets Act.

Pendock was now convinced that something disastrous had happened and made contact with two of his journalist friends, Marshall Pugh – the young Scot who had written Crabb's biography – and James Gleeson, who ran a news agency and wrote radio scripts; he was also co-author, with Tom Waldron, of *The Frogmen*.

Having known Crabb for many years even before he employed him as a furniture salesman, Pendock had been the first to hear of the intended Portsmouth trip. A month earlier, Crabb had said he would be 'doing another job for the Admiralty' at Portsmouth in mid-April and would need a couple of days off. As he had already talked of having dived under the Russian cruiser *Sverdlov* the previous October, it was quite clearly understood that he would be doing something similar this time. Crabb even said with a dirty chuckle, in his gravelly voice, 'I'll be having a look at the Russians' bottoms', and once he stopped Pendock in the street, pointed to a building about 50 yards away and said, 'That will be as far as I shall have to swim at Portsmouth.'

Pendock now confided his fears to the two journalist friends but they laughed and said, 'Crabbie will turn up. He always does.'

Knowing Crabb's real reason for going to Portsmouth, Pendock was reluctant to make a direct enquiry to the Admiralty. He expressed his worries to a woman he knew in the radio world: 'Tom Fallon's your man. He knows all about these mysterious things.' Tom Fallon was a former Scotland Yard superintendent who had left the force to write for radio; he agreed to make enquiries and to meet Pendock on the following Wednesday evening. There was no meeting, however, for Pendock received a telephone call to say that an Admiralty representative would be calling at about 5.00 pm.

Captain Richard Ivan Alexander Sarell, DSO, a senior Admiralty officer whose appointment on the staff of the Deputy Chief of Naval Staff forms a link with the Cabinet Office through the Ministry of Defence, arrived at Pendock's Seymour Place salesroom at the appointed time. He was in civilian clothes, and declined Pendock's suggestion that they should talk over a drink in a neighbouring hotel.

He said, 'Let's just walk.' Then he changed his mind and said, 'It would be better in my flat,' and they went to a bachelor flat in Dorset House, Gloucester Place. There the Captain, obviously ill at ease, asked, 'Did Commander Crabb tell you why he was going to Portsmouth?'

Pendock, obviously in a difficult position, said, 'No'.

The captain poured out a whisky and said, 'I'm sorry to have to tell you that he failed to surface after diving to test some new equipment. But I think we should keep it to ourselves. Give him a day or two, he may have been picked up by a fishing boat.'

What was Pendock to do? He had many journalist friends. Crabb was news, had been on and off for years, and he was a brave man whose passing deserved notice. But the Russian leaders were still in Britain. What would be the effect of news that a frogman was lost near Portsmouth, and what would happen if the truth came out?

Then a curious fact emerged: the Admiralty apparently did not know the address of Crabb's next of kin. The Captain asked where his wife lived, and Pendock explained that Crabb had no wife, as his marriage had been dissolved 18 months previously. He also told the officer about Crabb's fiancée but said that his mother would be his next of kin: he knew that she lived in Oxfordshire and said that if he had a map of the area he might be able to remember it. Sarell wrote down an

Admiralty extension number and gave it to Pendock. 'If you remember anything, please give me a ring. If I'm not there, I have a couple of junior officers who will take a message.' Sarell certainly stressed to Pendock that Crabb's disappearance should not be talked about, so Pendock explained that Crabb's biographer Marshall Pugh would need to be told. Sarell agreed but asked that he should be the one to tell him.

Pugh told Frank Goldsworthy that he did meet the Captain at the Dorset House flat, and he also came back impressed with the necessity of making no hurried move to release the news, saying, 'Crabbie would not want to embarrass the Navy.'

It was not until the following Friday that Pendock remembered the Oxfordshire village where Crabb's mother lived: Towersey, near Thame. He phoned the Admiralty extension number and was told that the Captain was not available but that he spent most of his time at the Ministry of Defence. Pendock was given another number, which he phoned, only to be told that the Captain was in conference so he left a message.

Pendock's call was returned later, and Sarell told him that he was going to drive down to see Crabb's mother and break the news to her. He said that he hated the prospect, and also stated that it had been decided that the news of Crabb's death could now be released. Pendock did not immediately connect the fact that Bulgarin and Khrushchev had departed, smiling broadly and waving cheerily from the bridge of the *Ordzhonikidze*, which had lain for nine days alongside the jetty at Portsmouth.

Captain Sarell later told Pendock that he had seen Crabb's mother and now intended to go down to Kent to see his former wife. Both women were to later describe the visit of the naval officer in civilian clothes. He was obviously ill at ease and unable to give a clear account of what might have happened, but said there might be hope if Crabb had been picked up by a fishing boat or a foreign vessel.

Sarell asked Pendock if he would call on the housekeeper where Crabb had his flat and say that he would not be returning. He also asked him to pay any outstanding bills and forward the receipts to the Admiralty who would reimburse him. He could offer no adequate explanation to be given to the housekeeper and Pendock refused to do it.

On the Sunday afternoon Marshall Pugh felt that it would be

ridiculous to keep the matter secret any longer. Crabb was well known to many people and there were cuttings filed about him in every newspaper library in Fleet Street. Pugh prepared a brief paragraph about Crabb's presumed death while engaged in underwater work, summarised his past exploits and added a note that a book about his life was awaiting publication. He then sat down at the telephone to dial Fleet Street numbers and tell the story of how Crabb had failed to surface ten days earlier. The news would send ripples right around the world.

When Pat Rose returned home, her landlord, Lloyd Pride, an Australian, said that a naval officer had called and left a message. He said that Crabb had gone missing whilst undertaking a diving job but that he might turn up or be found.

Pat was shattered, her worst fears a reality. She rang her brother in the south of France, and he advised her to pack her things and catch the next train. The following morning she was besieged by reporters, seeking the story that was to make world headlines. She did not speak to them for she was confused about the affair. She booked on to the blue train for France and went to stay with her brother.

During office hours, newspaper enquiries to the Admiralty were handled by the staff of the Chief of Naval Information. Unlike some Ministries, the Admiralty neither kept a late watch of information officers nor made the home telephone number of the stand-by man available to reporters. Instead, after 6.00 pm and on Sundays, press calls were switched to the duty commander who was provided with 'briefs' to cover subjects that were likely to arise out of office hours. He would be in touch with operational matters but occasional enquiries normally handled by the civilian side of the Admiralty were referred to the resident clerk. One anonymous civil servant (in fact it was an overnight duty shared in rotation by several responsible men) was to play a vital part in the Crabb story on the evening of Sunday 29 April.

Marshall Pugh's telephoned paragraph caught the eye of Fleet Street news editors. Here was a man whose exploits in many parts of the world had brought intermittent fame, and who was now reported to have been killed in unexplained circumstances in the service of his country.

The first call to the Admiralty was made by Bernard Hall of the *Daily Express*. The duty commander referred Hall to the resident clerk. Before him, when the phone rang in his office around tea time, was a typewritten brief prepared some days before by senior officers who knew that press enquiries would have to be dealt with sooner or later.

Now, if Crabb had disappeared on an espionage mission which would embarrass Britain and possibly endanger peace with Russia, this would have been the moment to produce a convincing lie; it was also the opportune time for the Admiralty to disclaim any involvement with a man who was reputedly a civilian. As it was, the brief merely contained details which it was hoped would play down the affair. He had no communiqué to issue as such, just points of information he was authorised to give.

Yes, he agreed, Commander Crabb was missing, presumed drowned, having failed to surface after a dive when experimenting with secret equipment.

'What sort of equipment?'

'Sorry, no information can be given about that.'

'Well, where did it happen?'

'In the Portsmouth area.'

'The Portsmouth area is a big place! – whereabouts?'

'Just in the Portsmouth area.'

'Well, when did it happen?'

'Oh, a week or so ago.'

He would say no more.

It took no great leap of the imagination for a journalist to remember that in Portsmouth, where this George Medallist frogman had been lost, a Russian cruiser and two Russian destroyers had been berthed 'a week or so ago'.

It was some time later when the resident clerk, after having taken other advice, agreed that he had also been authorised to say that the tests had been undertaken in Stokes Bay. This was the weak link in the story given out and it was the key statement that encouraged those seeking a story to delve deeper. If the original statement had been made with a little more conviction, with some mention of rescue attempts and the tidal currents which swept the bay, it might have satisfied the curiosity of the newspaper men. However, if newsmen are denied information from one source for no apparent reason, they have a habit of looking elsewhere for it.

At Portsmouth, nobody seemed to have heard of the disappearance of Commander Crabb, not even the underwater specialists who could have been expected to accompany and support him if he were called in as a sort of underwater expert on some new piece of equipment. Those who knew anything were long gone. Moreover, no boats had been called out to make a search, nor had the police been informed about a missing frogman.

Stokes Bay is about three miles away from where the Russian cruiser and destroyers lay in Portsmouth harbour. A boat is able to cross the shallows at high tide, and that is the shortest route. Following the deep water route would involve roughly a five-mile journey.

On Monday 30 April, the *Daily Sketch* reported:

'News of Crabb's death has been kept secret for a week, for security reasons. He made his last dive in Stokes Bay at Portsmouth, the scene of secret test trials, not far from the mooring place of the Russian ships which brought Bulganin and Khrushchev to this country. His dive was to test a most important hush-hush item of equipment developed by the Royal Navy.'

Four days later, when other evidence had made the Stokes Bay 'accident' look even less credible, the Soviet Ambassador in London found this newspaper report suitable for quotation in a surprisingly mild protest to the Foreign Office about a frogman having been seen near the Russian ships.

Whilst the newspapers took up the Stokes Bay story, another twist in the mystery arose. Bernard Hutton says in *The Fake Defector* that, on Sunday 29 April, a report was issued officially by Commander Blanders, the captain of a Danish destroyer. His ship had been shadowing the *Ordzhonikidze* and the two escorting destroyers when a helicopter landed on the cruiser. The Danish crew observed through binoculars that two men boarded the helicopter. One of the men was being 'led'. The radio officer aboard the Danish ship recorded two coded messages which were forwarded to a Soviet defector in Denmark, Igor Vutnovke, who was an expert on Russian ciphers. He decoded the message whose contents indicated that the helicopter was arriving to take off a prisoner and requested fighter cover, which was granted. Thus Denmark had officially stated that a prisoner was removed from the cruiser, by helicopter, the day before the British press announced that Crabb had died in Stokes Bay in Portsmouth.

Other newspapers took up the story on Monday morning. The *Daily Mail* reported that Crabb had died secretly in the waters of Stokes Bay, three miles from where the Russian warships were then lying in Portsmouth. The paper went on . . .

'Admiralty officials said last night that he had not been diving under the Russian ships to investigate their propellers and hull forms. The Russians had often had their own divers down during their stay and this was considered normal practice. Our own Navy does the same with its ships when in harbour.'

The first public connection between Crabb and the Russian ships had been made.

There might have been some excuse for the resident clerk, on duty alone on a Sunday night, being unable to amplify a casualty report, however well known the victim and however dramatic his presumed death. However, there was no reason why on Monday the entire Naval Information Department could give no more details. The pitiful reason given was that the equipment concerned was so secret that nothing could be revealed. This was insufficient to explain why no information should be given about rescue efforts, nor why former colleagues should have been kept so long in ignorance of the loss of an old friend.

The Admiralty would add nothing despite high level conferences and they remained intransigent for the next two weeks. They must have heaved a sigh of relief when they opened their newspapers on Tuesday morning. The *Daily Sketch* was offering an explanation that Crabb had been killed whilst examining a new pressure mine, in some 20 feet (6 m) of water, a mile offshore in Stokes Bay.

Nevertheless, the Crabb story did not die and was soon out of control as the press continued to seek out the truth. It came to light that Crabb had not been alone and the press turned its attention to 'Mr Smith'. Slowly a picture began to emerge of the man who had stayed with Commander Crabb at the Sally Port Hotel three weeks previously: the man who drove him there, who paid his hotel bill when he vanished; the man whose signature, it is reasonable to assume, was the thing which Whitehall wanted to hide when they asked Portsmouth CID to cut pages from the hotel register, and the man whose cheque Crabb carried to Portsmouth and which had disappeared.

A woman with a foreign accent, giving the name of Anderson, called at Pendock's furniture office. She asked to see one of the principals and was shown into an inner office, when she said she had come to settle the Smith account. She paid the bill with four consecutively-numbered one pound notes, N77 J 241274 to N77 J 241277, and a ten shilling note, also new, C 47 Z 720396.

The incident was noticed by a reporter, who followed the woman. She dodged through the busy hallway of the Cumberland Hotel, jumped on a bus, got off at the next stop, stood waiting in a queue, then suddenly slipped away in the crowd.

The uproar in Parliament that followed the announcement of Commander Crabb's disappearance was understandable, for both the House of Commons and the general public wanted to know the truth. The Admiralty said one thing whilst the media said another. Questions were asked but the replies given did not satisfy public interest, nor have answers been provided over the ensuing years.

At that time the Prime Minister, Sir Anthony Eden, had forbidden any form of covert operations to be undertaken against the Russian visitors, but elements of the British and American secret service had decided that the visit was too good an opportunity to miss. The British were aware that the Russians would be watching for Crabb as they knew about his underwater exploits, such as that under the *Sverdlov* during her own visit. The Russians also had valuable assistance from their agents within MI5 and MI6. Who those people were has subsequently come to light and, in an attempt to cover their identification, many writers have been stopped from printing details of the spy network which was an embarrassment to the British authorities. Chapman Pincher has in his books on the British Secret Service indicated that the leak could have come from Sir Roger Hollis who became Director General of MI5 and who was involved with the Crabb operation. Indeed, he may well have been the controller who arranged Crabb's infiltration and capture. Hollis came under suspicion, but as late as 1981 was declared innocent in Parliament. Reports still abound to indicate that he was the likeliest source of any leak from the British secret service at that period.

The first ripple in the political pond had begun on the day of the incident when the commander of the Soviet ships, Rear Admiral V.F.

Kotov, reported to the chief of staff of Portsmouth Naval Base, Rear Admiral Philip Burnett, that 'At about 7.30 am on 19 April, sailors on watch aboard the Soviet ships had observed a frogman floating on the surface between the ships. The frogman stayed on the surface for a short time before submerging out of sight.' Burnett knew about the ban on any intelligence-gathering involvement against the Soviet ships but stated that he knew nothing about any covert underwater operations, nor could he give any indication about the identity of the frogman.

But that same evening the subject was raised again. Jamie Thomas, the First Lord of the Admiralty, was at a dinner with the Soviet officials from the ships when he was asked, 'What was that frogman doing off our bows this morning?' Thomas was taken aback at the question, and could only reply that he knew nothing about any frogman, nor his identity. He stated that whoever it was was there without authorisation and was certainly not a member of the Royal Navy.

The following day saw the first of several high-level secret meetings begin in Whitehall, with the purpose of organising a cover-up. Help came from an unexpected quarter when a row between the guests of honour, Bulgarin and Khrushchev, and the two Labour Party leaders, Hugh Gaitskell and George Brown, erupted at a dinner organised by the Labour Party Executive Committee. This was well covered by the media, and provided a welcome distraction. But by Sunday 29 April – ten days after Crabb's disappearance – friends of the Commander were asking very leading questions. The authorities had not expected the reaction to be so great, nor that many of those enquiring would be involved with Fleet Street: Crabb's reputation as a loner without many friends was beginning to backfire. Those who had sent Crabb on the mission had miscalculated.

Eventually the Admiralty issued a statement to the effect that Commander Lionel Crabb was missing presumed dead, having failed to return from a test dive connected with trials of certain underwater apparatus in Stokes Bay. This statement was pure fabrication on the part of the Admiralty who were trying to delay the media linking Crabb's disappearance with the visit of the Soviet ships. It soon became apparent that the statement was simply an attempt to save embarrassment in Westminster and Whitehall.

The media reported the statement but began their own investigations into the affair. They were soon to see through the cover-up. The Russian leaders, now back in the Soviet Union, saw the possibility of making political capital out of the débâcle and on 4 May issued the following note to the British Authorities, as quoted in full in Hansard on 30 May:

'The Embassy of the Union of Soviet Socialist Republics in Great Britain presents its compliments to the Foreign Office and has the honour to state as follows:

'During the stay of the Soviet warships at Portsmouth at 7.30 hours on 19 April, three sailors of the Soviet vessels discovered a diver swimming between the Soviet destroyers at their moorings at the South Railway jetty. The diver, dressed in a black light-diving suit with flippers on his feet, was on the surface of the water for the space of one or two minutes and then dived again under the destroyer "Smotryashchie".

'The Commander of the Soviet warships, Rear Admiral V.F. Kotov, in conversation with the chief of staff of the Portsmouth naval base, Rear Admiral Burnett, drew attention to the fact of the appearance of the diver near the anchorages of the Soviet vessels, immediately alongside the destroyers.

'Rear Admiral Burnett categorically denied the possibility of the appearance of a diver alongside the Soviet vessels and declared that at the time no diving operations of any kind were being carried out. In reality, however, as appears from information reported in the British press of 30 April last, there is confirmation of the fact that the British naval authorities were actually carrying out secret diving investigations in the vicinity of the anchored Soviet vessels at Portsmouth. Moreover, the carrying out of these investigations caused a fatality to a British diver. It is sufficient to quote that the "Daily Sketch" in reporting the loss of the diver Crabb, stated as follows:

' "He went into the water for the last time at Stokes Bay, Portsmouth, on secret investigatory work near to the anchorage of the Soviet cruiser 'Ordzhonikidze'."

'Attaching as it does important significance to such an unusual occurrence as the Soviet warships visiting the British naval base at Portsmouth, the Embassy would be grateful to the British Foreign Office to receive an explanation on the question.
London, 4 May, 1956.'

The Foreign Office responded to the Soviet complaint and sent the following note of explanation and apology:

'The Foreign Office presents its compliments to the Embassy of the Union of Soviet Socialist Republics and has the honour to make the following reply to the Embassy's note of 4 May.

As has already been publicly announced, Commander Crabb was engaged in diving tests and is presumed to have met his death whilst so engaged.

The diver, who stated in the Soviet note was observed from the Soviet warships to be swimming between the Soviet destroyers, was presumably Commander Crabb. His approach to the destroyers was completely unauthorised and Her Majesty's Government desire to express their regret at the incident.

Foreign Office, SW1.

9 May, 1956.'

Even though the British authorities had tried to keep the Crabb affair secret, some details were made public on the same day of the note, 4 May, when Gordon Holman of the London *Evening Standard* reported that he had telephoned the Soviet Embassy to ask for any information they might have to help clear up the mystery of the disappearance of Commander Crabb in Portsmouth. The reporter spoke to an assistant naval attaché who said that his name should not be quoted and then went on to describe the incident in Portsmouth. He said: 'A watchman in our ship saw a frogman come to the surface in Portsmouth harbour. He was on the surface for only a few seconds. Then he disappeared and was not seen again. The watchman reported seeing the frogman to the captain of the warships.' The reporter asked if any action was taken against the frogman. The assistant naval attaché answered, 'Absolutely none. We were in a British port and there was nothing we could do. Action in such a case is forbidden in our Navy.'

The information that the authorities had been trying to hide now came out into the open.

The Opposition party who had fared so poorly during their meeting with the Soviet leaders now had the upper hand, and they used their advantage to the maximum. Sir Anthony Eden, who was outraged when the news was first presented to him, now had to face demanding questions from the opposition benches. To make matters worse, the security services had operated without his knowledge or consent, and against his direct orders.

On 9 May, Sir Anthony Eden told a full House of Commons that 'It would not be in the public interest to disclose the circumstances in which Commander Crabb is presumed to have met his death. While it is the practice for Ministers to accept responsibility I think it necessary, in the special circumstances of this case, to make it clear that what was done was done without the authority or the knowledge of Her Majesty's Ministers. Appropriate disciplinary steps are being taken.' Sir Anthony put down on the despatch box in front of him the paper from which he read those words. He had his palms outstretched, firmly clasping the corners of the despatch box. His voice and face were solemn and expressionless. 'What was done, was done! What was known was known!'

There was uproar from the Opposition who demanded detailed explanations and wanted to know whom the Prime Minister was shielding. Five times Sir Anthony was asked for more details and five times the same answer was given in different words, that the Prime Minister would add nothing further.

Before making his speech, the Prime Minister had received a report from naval intelligence and the secret service who revealed details of the operation to him.

He had to make the basis of his speech from the information with which he was provided. It is evident that what the Prime Minister received by way of explanation from the relevant authorities was far too sensitive to be explained or debated in Parliament. The operation was therefore more far-reaching and complex than a frogman swimming under or near the Soviet warships to 'have a look'.

Was the Prime Minister presented with details of a daring plan to put Crabb into the Soviet Union, to seek out vital information in the interest of national security? If he was, then the statements and answers he gave to Parliament were in order. It was probably at this point that MI5 began to investigate the background of Maitland Pendock. They found that many of his acquaintances were affiliated to the Communist Party and they would have discovered that he also knew members of MI5 and MI6. From this it could be deduced that, if his business was not a clearing house for those departments, it was certainly the most likely place for a security breakdown on the Crabb operation.

Sir Anthony was obviously faced with the embarrassment that a covert operation had taken place against his direct orders, and could have divulged more information to his closest Ministers, if not Parliament in general, but he chose not to do so. Was he faced with the facts that Commander Crabb had been sent on a dangerous mission, to be put in on the other side, but had been double-crossed by members of the British security service who had allegiance to the Soviet Union? Did he know that Crabb was trapped and could not be got out, and that the Russians were playing cat and mouse with a major prize?

An interesting point in the Parliamentary debates, which were noisy and prolonged, was that one former Labour Minister who knew most about security, Mr Herbert Morrison, had removed himself from the scene and took no part in the harassment of the Prime Minister. Did he have some knowledge of what had happened but felt that the matter should be left? He would have been unable to have stated such for the Opposition was out for blood.

Mr Gaitskell for the Opposition told the Prime Minister that his speech was totally unsatisfactory and asked whether he was 'aware that, while all of us would wish to protect public security, the suspicion must inevitably arise that his refusal to make a statement on this subject is not so much in the interest of public security as to hide a very grave blunder which has occurred?'

To this the Prime Minister replied that the House and the country could draw their own conclusions from what he had said. He added that he had anxiously weighed every consideration, but these were decisions which only a Prime Minister could take and he was convinced that the decision he had taken was 'the right and only one'.

This again highlights the fact that the Crabb operation was more significant than a frogman having a look under a Russian ship. At the time this in itself would certainly have been embarrassing, but not sufficiently to explain the constant questioning and barracking that he received on the matter. The subject would not go away and the Opposition delivered questions from every angle. The next demand came from Mr 'Manny' Shinwell who wanted to know against whom the disciplinary action was being taken and for what reason. Sir Anthony was reluctant to answer but there were fierce demands for a reply. He rose to the box, clasped it determinedly and said 'I have nothing to add to the answer I have given'.

Whilst there was no change from the Prime Minister, there were changes in the security services. The disciplinary procedure started at the top and the chief of MI6, Major General Sir John 'Sindbad' Sinclair, was retired early to be replaced by the man who was serving as the Director General of MI5, Sir Dick White. Roger Hollis was promoted.

The Russians saw the turmoil that the Crabb affair had caused in Britain and exploited it to the full. They made their displeasure known through every source. In an interview with Admiral Kotov, *Pravda* related that: 'On 19 April at 7.30 am, three sailors from the destroyer *Sovershenny*, moored alongside the cruiser *Ordzhonikidze* in Portsmouth harbour, noticed a diver in a black lightweight diving suit on the surface of the water between the Soviet destroyers . . . For some time the diver remained on the surface face upwards, then he submerged by the hull of the destroyer *Smotryaschie* . . .' If, as was stated by the Russians, Crabb lay on the surface *face up* for some time, where he could be observed, he would have compromised a routine surveillance operation and would have aborted the dive. He clearly remained on the surface to ensure that the lookout (who he knew were watching) would observe him.

If a diver on a covert operation needs to surface to have a look above the water, he does so leaving the minimum amount of his head exposed and in this case would have tried to do so under the lee of the ships. When submerging, he would dip down gently without causing any flurry of water or splashing. He would never expose his fins (flippers) – yet the observers noted 'rubber flippers'. The actions reported are not the actions of a diver in trouble but of one making sure that he was observed. The fact that he was operating in daylight underlines this conclusion.

The Crabb controversy continued to rage unabated in the House of Commons where the Opposition still demanded more answers than those so far given. However, on 14 May the House of Commons, after a heated and turbulent debate, approved by 316 votes to 229 the veil of secrecy which the Prime Minister had deemed necessary to draw over the Commander Crabb affair.

Sir Anthony's ten-minute speech never once mentioned the frogman by name and provided no further insight into the subject. It ended with a final declaration: 'In this business I do not rest only on the national interest . . . there is also in this business a very important international interest, and I confess that all I care for is the outcome of our discussions with the Soviet leaders, should this in truth prove to be, as I have said, the beginning of a beginning. I intend to safeguard that possibility at all costs. I believe that that is also in the mind of the Soviet leaders, and it is for that reason that I deplore this debate and will say no more.'

Mr Hugh Gaitskell for the Opposition, who had opened the debate, had also earlier raised the matter of the pages of the hotel register which had been removed in a manner no more legal than was threatening the staff with the Official Secrets Act. The question was asked, 'Can the Prime Minister tell us under what authority these officers acted?' It remained unanswered.

From the question laid before the Prime Minister, and the total lack of answers provided, it is apparent that people in high office were aware of and had authorised the Crabb operation. The Prime Minister was deeply impressed by the report of the operation, which was sufficiently serious that he did not discuss it with any of his Cabinet Ministers and carried the responsibility alone.

In the Soviet Union, Crabb's capture was being celebrated with a gold watch being presented to Admiral Kotov, who had brought Bulganin and Khrushchev to Portsmouth. This happened at the end of May 1956 and Western observers were certain that it was a reward for the smooth diving operation that had enabled Crabb to be captured and taken aboard the cruiser. The watch was presented by Marshall Zhukov, Soviet Minister of Defence. Captain G.F. Stephanov, commander of the *Ordzhonikidze*, also received a gold watch for his part in the operation. The official reason for the awards was as recognition of the two commanders who distinguished themselves during their stay in England.

The Russians had initially encouraged the fiasco that had developed within the House of Commons and in the media. When evidence began to emerge to the effect that Crabb had been captured and taken as a prisoner to the Soviet Union they became perturbed and issued statements to the effect that the British were 'rattling skeletons in the cupboard' in an attempt to cover up a security scandal. They went on to declare that Commander Crabb had 'perished' whilst engaged in underwater espionage against the Soviet cruiser. That was a very damaging statement to make, for the vast majority of people did not know what had happened to Commander Crabb and those who did were not saying. Was this an indirect way of saying to the British authorities that Commander Lionel Crabb had 'perished' but was now living under a new name, Lev Lvovich Korablov, and working for the Russians?

Much has been made of what Commander Crabb was looking for when he went under the ship. In view of the earlier *Sverdlov* mission, there could have been no reason to risk another operation on a sister ship. Moreover, only six years after the incident, in 1962, the *Ordzhonikidze* was transferred to the Indonesian Navy where she was renamed the *Kri Irian**. This would hardly have happened if she had really been one of the most modern warships in the world!

Any superior capabilities that the vessel displayed would have been noticed by Captain Northey of the Royal Navy, who travelled from the Soviet Union to Portsmouth with the Russian party. He had every door open to him, and saw everything there was to see. He was allowed to mix with the officers and crew. So there was no need for underwater spies – but then Crabb was not spying against the ship.

The Admiralty maintained its account of the Stokes Bay incident and this drew much attention to the fact that there must be a 'cover-up' which was going wrong. If Commander Crabb were indeed on active naval service in Stokes Bay on 19 April 1956, experimenting with a new secret mine, he would have embarked on his mission from HMS *Vernon* or another naval establishment and would have been taken to the starting point in some naval craft, since Stokes Bay is more than three miles from Portsmouth harbour. Moreover, if he was carrying out a top-secret underwater experiment with a new type of mine, why did Sir Anthony tell a thoroughly aroused House of Commons that 'It would not be in the public interest to disclose the circumstances in which Commander Crabb is presumed to have met his death?' He also added, 'I think it necessary, in the special circumstances of this case, to make it clear that what was done was done without the authority or the knowledge of Her Majesty's Ministers. Appropriate disciplinary steps are being taken.'

*The *Ordzhonikidze* was found to have no bow propellor, or other underwater devices, but the *Sverdlov*, which is still in service in the Soviet navy, did.

Secret experiments with new weapons are not dependent on special authority from Her Majesty's Ministers so why should 'appropriate disciplinary steps' need to be taken? Even if in the public interest and for security reasons Sir Anthony could not disclose that the test of a very special secret weapon had taken place, he should have been able to say more than he did and would not have exposed himself to unnecessary sharp attacks from his own side of the House as well as from the Opposition. And if Crabb had been killed when a mine unexpectedly exploded, why did the official Admiralty announcement state, 'He is presumed to be dead' and why did ten days elapse before the official proclamation was made?

If Crabb had been in Stokes Bay carrying out Royal Navy orders some three miles from the berth at which the Soviet cruiser lay at anchor, why did Sir Anthony tell the House during the resumed debate – with great vehemence – that all he cared for was that the outcome of the discussions with the Soviet leaders should, in truth, prove to be the beginning of the beginning and add: 'I intend to safeguard that possibility at all costs'? Routine naval experiments miles away from the Soviet flotilla could hardly have impaired talks with the Russian leaders in any way.

When the KGB officer Anatoli Golitsin defected in Finland during the early 1960s he provided his interrogators with more than a hundred leads on past and present agents. He said that he had read scores of NATO documents sent by agents to Moscow. As part of the investigation he was provided with genuine and bogus papers, for which he picked out the right ones. He had indeed seen secret NATO papers. He also gave details of how Soviet naval intelligence knew that Crabb was to make the dive and had planned his capture. He said that, through information received by agents, the Russians had details of the planned dive and captured him alongside the ships. The operation was known to a Soviet agent at a fairly high level in MI5 or MI6. Facts revealed by Golitsin on other matters proved to be reliable so there was no reason to doubt the information about Crabb.

Harry Houghton, who served a 15-year prison sentence for spying whilst he worked at the Underwater Weapons Establishment at Portland, stated in his book *Operation Portland* that Crabb was captured by Russian divers and taken into the cruiser through a wet compartment. He also claims that Crabb gave some details of the operation he was to have carried out and then died. The Russians, unable to return him to the British, deposited his body in the water when the Soviet ships left port.

During questioning about his spying activities, Houghton tried to do a deal but this was not accepted and so many of his statements should be regarded with some scepticism. He is also reputed to have deliberately created some mystery in the book he published in order to enhance its readership.

Apart from the reports that were raised throughout the ensuing years, Parliament had not heard the last of the matter. Amongst those who took up the 'truth about Crabb' challenge was Commander J.S. Kerans, DSO, RN (Retd), who had been on HMS *Amethyst* when she withstood the bombardment by the Chinese and escaped from the Yangtse River. As Member of Parliament for Hartlepool, he made a very bold statement in 1960: 'I am convinced that Commander Lionel Crabb is alive and in Russian hands – the Government must re-open this case.'

Commander Kerans tabled a question in the House of Commons asking the then Foreign Secretary, Mr Selwyn Lloyd, to start new enquiries into the case of the British frogman, Commander Crabb, who had vanished when diving near the Soviet ships. He based his evidence upon the research undertaken by Bernard Hutton. Kerans discussed the details of his report with naval friends, who had experience of espionage work. As a result he stated, 'I do not believe this [Hutton's research] is a fabrication'.

But Kerans, as others before him, received no satisfaction for the Crabb affair was firmly closed.

In 1964, Marcus Lipton, Labour Member for Brixton, submitted new evidence to Mr Harold Wilson, the Prime Minister. The information he placed before him was based on statements made by a high-ranking official who was linked with British and American intelligence. This official helped to investigate the Crabb mystery. The statements revealed that British intelligence had received reports seven years previously, indicating that Crabb was in Russia.

Marcus Lipton supported the report by saying, 'I know the name of the British official who disclosed this information and to whom he disclosed it. I also know when and where the conversations took place. There is at least a circumstantial case for another look at the affair.'

Harold Wilson studied the report and would have consulted the appropriate authorities to seek advice on the matter. From the facts presented to him he decided, as had his predecessors, not to make any statement. It is of interest to note that although Labour Members of Parliament had made demands for the truth at the time of the incident, now, eight years after the event when they were in power, they would not reveal the facts.

Mr Wilson wrote to Colonel Lipton, MP: 'I have read the enclosures, but I am afraid I do not think they provide grounds for re-opening this case.' Colonel Lipton told the Press: 'I am sorry speculation about this mystery is to be allowed to continue. I am convinced that one day the whole truth will come out.'

Another MP, Bernard Floud, Labour Member for Acton, saw Hutton's 'dossier' and, through a friend in MI6, confirmed that the dossier matched one held by British intelligence. He also declared that he had confirmed the details provided by the two naval officers at HMS *Vernon*. Other items of supporting evidence put forward by him included a de-coded Soviet message, reporting the capture of a frogman in Portsmouth harbour. For the disbelievers of the 'Crabb in Russia' theory, the evidence was substantial. For Hutton, it was the final proof he needed, but in 1967 Floud was exposed as a Soviet agent. He had been recruited by the KGB during his time at Oxford University. MI5 officers began a series of interrogations, which resulted in Floud's committing suicide. Another piece of the Crabb jigsaw had fallen by the wayside.

The fact remains that the truth has never been revealed by any prime minister. Every one must have cause to look at the secret file, and every one has decided never to disclose the contents. On 1 January 1987, many documents were made public for the first time under the 30-year rule but nothing relating to the Crabb mystery. It seems likely that it will remain buried a 100 years.

7

The Search

When Syd Knowles heard the details of Crabb's disappearance he was
outraged that no proper search had been made for his friend. If Crabb
was reported missing surely somebody, either military or civilian,
should have carried out some form of search, but nothing happened.
Knowles decided that, if the authorities were unconcerned, he was
not, and so he set out for Portsmouth to search for the Commander.
Portsmouth Harbour is a very large expanse of water and Knowles
watched the movement of the tides and currents. He found an area
of water where the current washed up anything moving with the tide,
and decided that if Crabb's body was anywhere it could be in the
quiet area. He prepared his equipment and made a dive. Swimming
amongst the mud and flotsam of Portsmouth harbour he made a
thorough search, but found nothing.

Knowles prepared to make another dive but was approached by a
serving officer, who told him not to dive again, because Crabb's body
was not there. He said that he knew a lot about the secret operation
but could not elaborate for fear of the Official Secrets Act. Knowles
knew the officer and realised that he was not being fobbed off, knew
that Crabb would not be found by diving, so he abandoned his attempts
and returned home.

Harry Cole of Emsworth, near Portsmouth, was out fishing in
Chichester harbour in November 1956. It was dark and he was alone.
As he drew a trawl with iron shoes through the water, he felt a tug
on the equipment which suggested that he had caught something quite
large in the net. He began the slow process of hauling the trawl to

the boat and, as it reached the surface, saw a large object in it.

Groping in the darkness, he grabbed hold of the thing and attempted to find out what it was. He realised that it was rubber and as he struggled with it he found, to his horror, that he was holding a human head. It had come away from the body. He let go of the head, which fell back into the water to sink out of sight. However he kept hold of a piece of rubber tubing which had a mouthpiece that looked like a metal buckle, and part of a rubber belt, which was obviously part of a frogman's outfit. He then released the body from the trawl and let it sink into the murky waters.

Cole took a compass bearing of his location and returned home. He reported the incident to the police on 7 February 1957, stating that he had found the body on or about 3 November 1956, but because of the tide movements and his delay in reporting the incident the police did not take any action. The reason for Cole's delay in reporting his find only emerged later.

Cole is reputed to have told one investigator, who cannot be named, that he had the body on the surface but could not drag the body into the boat because it was far too heavy. He stated that the body still had underwater breathing apparatus on it and he was able to draw a rather accurate sketch of that equipment. He also describes small pouches on the front and back of the vest which held round weights. It was reported that he kept the weights aboard the boat and used them as part of his fishing gear.

This information is puzzling in two respects: first in the fact that Cole was able to describe and draw a sketch of generally unfamiliar equipment, when the incident apparently happened when it was dark and he was alone in the boat. He was unable to get the body into the boat but managed to turn the body over to look at breathing equipment. It would appear that he must have held the body for some time, making a good examination before letting it go.

The most alarming thing, though, if Cole's story is true, is that the equipment he examined and is reputed to have taken items from was British Royal Navy issue. The equipment Crabb owned and always used was Italian, and had no weight pouch and no ball weights; divers using the Italian apparatus wore a weight belt. Sydney Knowles stands by the fact that Crabb rarely used any other equipment and other naval divers state that Crabb had his own Italian breathing set and diving suit, and did not like to use the British equipment. The breathing equipment removed from HMS *Vernon* was of Italian manufacture.

Vital questions remain. If Cole found a body, whose was it, how did he manage to draw a detailed sketch of the equipment from an examination made in the dark, and how did he obtain the weights? It is another part of the Crabb jigsaw which does not fit, for why, in the wake of the Crabb incident, did the police take no action?*

The official view remained unaltered and any enquiries were met by the formal answer: 'The Admiralty has no comment, no further information and is not prepared to answer any questions at all.' The naval spokesman at Portsmouth declared that they had no knowledge of anything concerning the disappearance of Commander Crabb in the Portsmouth Command. Officially, the Crabb affair was closed.

Patricia Rose was still staying with her brother James and her sister-in-law Naomi in the south of France when a family friend, Tony Kessler, a former Austrian cavalry officer, phoned them and asked to speak to Pat. He told her that he was looking at an East German newspaper and that it had two photographs of her in it. She thought he was joking. He described the first one, of her standing with her brother and sister-in-law, both dressed in riding clothes, at their villa. Pat was shocked. He then told her that the other photograph was of her wearing shorts and sitting next to a swimming pool. Pat could not believe it, and Kessler told her that he would bring the paper to show her.

The three members of the family looked at the photographs, unbelieving, for they certainly were of them. The caption beside the photographs read: 'The beautiful blonde fiancée of Commander Crabb, the British frogman, who disappeared when the Soviet warships visited Britain on a goodwill visit. She is also missing.' The text gave strong indications that Crabb had defected to Russia and that she had followed him. How had the East Germans got hold of the photographs? The family had a set and these were still in their photograph album. Crabb had had a set and they were the same ones he had looked at on the train. The photographs that belonged to Crabb must have been the

*Harry Cole told his story more fully in a recent interview (recounted in a later chapter) which provides some, but not all, of the answers.

ones used, for they were not in his wallet when it was returned by the Admiralty to his mother with his other belongings, taken from the hotel room by Smith.

Pat Rose received many messages over the years, reputedly coming from underground sources in the East and Russia. The first contact came one day whilst she was out. When she returned to the villa, Joseph, the manservant, told her that there had been a message for her. He said that a man had asked to speak to her but, when told that she was out, he left a message. He stated that Commander Crabb was alive and well and that she would see him in ten years' time. He had a strange accent, and would leave no name or contact address.

She herself answered the phone the next time contact was made. The stranger asked to speak to Pat Rose. When she identified herself he repeated the message that Commander Crabb was alive and well. She then demanded to know who the man was, and asked if it was some sort of horrible joke. The man remained calm and replied that it was no joke. He told her that Crabb was being held at Lefortowo prison and that, if he worked for the Russians for ten years, he would be free to go wherever he wanted and that she would be re-united with him. Pat then asked the identity of the caller again – the phone went dead.

For Pat Rose it was a nightmare; she did not know whether the calls were hoaxes or whether they were genuine, for she knew that strange things happened under such circumstances and people could be very cruel.

Another caller telephoned the villa at Biot and spoke to her. Once he had assured himself that he was speaking to Pat, he told her that Commander Crabb was alive. She demanded to know who the caller was and asked why she should believe him. The man said that he was to remind her of a certain train journey to Portsmouth, when Crabb had studied the photographs he kept in his wallet. He also said that they were alone in the compartment. These statements were fact and she listened to the man. He said that Crabb hoped that all of her doubts about his being alive were now dispelled and that she was not to worry about him any longer; then the phone went dead.

Whilst Pat Rose was in France receiving her messages, a bottle was washed ashore in England. It was sealed and undamaged. Inside was a note reputedly from Commander Crabb addressed to his mother. The note was passed to Mrs Beatrice Crabb, who confirmed that the handwriting was that of her son Lionel. The content of the note is not known, and the question as to whether it could have been forged must have the simple answer, yes! It would have needed to be cleverly done to pass the scrutiny of those who examined it but one must ask why anybody should want to produce a forged document, for it could produce no conceivable result.

Two months after the Admiralty statement a French left-wing politician returned from Moscow and made a dramatic statement to the West German newspaper, *Bild Zeitung*, that Commander Lionel Crabb, the British frogman, was in fact alive, was being held in Moscow's Lefortowo prison, and that his prison number was 147. He continued to declare that Crabb had been captured in Portsmouth whilst investigating an automatic steering mechanism which enabled the Soviet vessels to manoueuvre quickly, and that Crabb had been offered a place in the Soviet Navy.

It was the 29 June edition of the *Bild* newspaper that revealed through 'dependable and secret sources' in the form of a high-ranking Soviet official, that Crabb was in Moscow. When asked about Crabb's capture the official explained that they had the right to arrest him as he was in the water close to the Soviet ship, which they considered to be Soviet territory. Crabb had been removed from the water, arrested and taken to the Soviet Union for questioning, where he may have been placed on trial for spying. The official confirmed that Crabb was held at Moscow's Lefortowo Prison and to ensure secrecy he was only known by a number which was confirmed as being 147.

The official made a further dramatic disclosure in that the officer in charge of Crabb's case had offered him a position in the Soviet secret service and that they wanted him to enter a special department of the Soviet Navy, to serve for ten years, which was the length of the prison sentence he would receive for espionage.

According to the official, Crabb had asked his captors to request authorisation from the British Government, allowing him to work for the Soviets. The *Bild* correspondent was told that this was obviously unacceptable, for the Soviets would not admit officially that they had captured Crabb, and the British authorities would never become embroiled in what could become an international incident.

Bild newspaper correspondents continued to pursue the story and spoke to Russian sailors ashore in Copenhagen, Denmark, who stated that a British frogman had been captured and had returned to the Soviet Union, held in the hospital of the *Ordzhonikidze*, which was closed to the crew during the journey back to the Soviet Union.

An article in the Soviet magazine *Sowjetfotte* gave brief details of the Crabb operation, stating that he had wanted to examine the underside of the Soviet cruiser, but it provided no details of his capture by Russian frogmen. It did however declare that Moscow had evidence which revealed that Crabb had been working for the American secret service and not the British. This revelation could have been a Soviet disinformation operation, designed to cause friction between the British and Americans.

The press did not let the subject rest and pursued every lead. Reuter issued a statement from the *Narodny Trudovoy Soyuz* (The People's League), who are Russians devoted to the destruction of the Communist system by establishing active cells within the Soviet Union. They have provided much genuine information and so are a credible source of information. They had learned from sailors who were aboard the cruiser when it visited Britain that somebody very important, but unknown to them, had been held in the hospital of the vessel and that no member of the crew was allowed near the area.

NTS is one of the oldest and most established opposition groups within the Soviet Union, and probably constitutes the greatest threat to the Communist Party of the Soviet Union. Their anti-Soviet activities were so extensive that the authorities ordered that a leader of NTS, Vladimir Poremsky, be assassinated. The act was not carried out, and even today the organisation's activities provide a steady flow of accurate information from within the USSR.

It was to NTS that we turned. In the organisation's booklet, NTS reveals that in June 1956 KGB officers Donchenko and Koretzky pretended to be seamen sympathising with NTS work, and attempted to lure the NTS operative in Antwerp aboard a soviet vessel. The two KGB men were in fact members of a special group which had been created in Leningrad to combat NTS infiltration of seamen of the Baltic fleet. It is little wonder that the KGB were concerned, for

NTS have confirmed from their records that a Soviet sailor from a military ship stated that he saw Commander Crabb alive. The NTS representatives in London had to resort to their archives in Europe, from which they were able to confirm that the details recorded about Crabb were substantiated.

In November 1959, Bernard Hutton, the author who delved into the Crabb affair and who produced a number of books about Crabb's being in Russia, obtained a secret dossier. He claimed that it came through underground contacts which he had and which were written in Russian and, when translated, described in detail Crabb's capture and interrogation. It covered the period when Crabb was invited to join the Red Navy. He was in fact offered two choices: join the Navy or be disposed of, as a spy. He chose the former. He was then given an identity as Lev Lvovich Korablov.

Hutton asked Syd Knowles what he thought about his latest book and in particular the dossier and photographs. Syd thought for a few moments and then said:

'There is one point in your book I just can't get. I can't see Crabbie learning Russian. Being in so many countries with Crabbie and learning a smattering of so many languages while we were together, Crabbie was such a damn bad learner.' Hutton disagreed and said that he had checked his facts so well, and insisted that Crabb had learnt Chinese. Syd said that his French was atrocious and his Italian was bad. After 12 months, Syd spoke fluent Italian but Crabb had only learnt odd phrases. Hutton insists that he was taught from morning to night until he could speak Russian. Syd accepted that if Crabb had learnt Chinese then it was possible that he had learnt Russian. Hutton also added that, in every report coming from Crabb/Korablov, he is credited with having a non-Russian accent.

Hutton had a vital piece of good luck when, after details of the dossier were published, he was contacted by the former head of MI5, Sir Percy Sillitoe, KBE, who examined it carefully before confirming that the contents were the same as those in the one held by the Secret Intelligence Service, apart from minor discrepancies which could have been caused during the translation. This was substantial evidence in the case for Crabb being alive in Russia.

Vital evidence began to appear in the form of photographs. In May

1960 one photograph of four Soviet naval officers arrived in the West. Bernard Hutton began to investigate the possibilities that one of the officers was Crabb. He had a problem since Crabb's mother was now dead and Patricia Rose was still in France, but the former Mrs Crabb was in England. Hutton met her and showed the photograph, asking if she recognised anybody in it. After careful consideration and study, she indicated the one named Korablov and said that it looked like Crabb, but she was not certain. The next person to be shown the photograph was Mr Edward Richman, the proprietor of the Sally Port Hotel in Portsmouth. He also picked out the same officer as being Crabb, although, since he had only seen Crabb briefly during his stay, his choice is not conclusive. Chief Petty Officer Ralph Thorpe, BEM, Crabb's diving instructor and close friend, is also said by Hutton to have chosen the one identified as Crabb.

Hutton then asked Syd Knowles about the photographs and Syd said categorically that the photographs of the Russian by the anti-aircraft gun was definitely *not* Crabb. 'No way. The person in that picture is far too young. No, it is not Crabbie.'

'What about the one on the ice?'

This was a photograph depicting a man standing on the ice at the East German naval base near Holtenhagen. Only half the face is visible since the photograph is damaged.

Syd said that, if any of the photographs depicted Crabbie, then that one was the most likely.

In a recent interview with Syd, he told me that he had looked at the pictures and thought about them for a long time and ruled out any chance of their being Commander Crabb.

It was in the early 1960s that the name of Maitland Pendock came to the forefront again. The case did not rest as far as he was concerned and he stated in 1960 that, after Captain Sarell had completed his official foray, two men confronted him and announced that they were from MI5. They produced their identity cards but kept their thumbs over their names. They said that they wished to ask him some questions and took him to a flat in Paddington. The two men then told Pendock in detail about his friends, the West End clubs he visited and places that he had been with Commander Crabb. They told him that they knew about his friendship with a leading Canadian Communist and asked what views Commander Crabb had about the present Government.

Pendock was frightened and no doubt wondered what Commander Crabb had been up to, and he answered in truth that he was a Conservative and although he had been friends with the Communist, he held no belief in his politics. As for the Commander, he was an ardent monarchist, often to extremes. Pendock was allowed to go home but, still frightened, he told his wife of the incident, saying that he must not talk about Commander Crabb because of the Official Secrets Act. Two days later another two men from MI5 called to see Pendock at his office and put the same types of question to him but phrased in a different way.

Pendock had to go on business to Ireland but when he returned home, he arrived in a state of shock. He told his wife that he had been visited by another two men, questioned and beaten. He showed her the bruising. He did not know who they were but they wanted to know what Crabb had told him about the job he was to do in Portsmouth, and whom he had told about it. Shortly after this incident Pendock travelled to Ireland, where he died – in what Pendock's own son has described to us as 'suspicious circumstances'.

It now emerged that Pendock's wife had Crabb's famous swordstick at their home. She did not know how it had got there. Were MI5 looking for a Communist leak that had put a British agent in position where they could not get him out?

A newspaper reporter claimed to have spoken to the officer on 'duty watch' with the petty officer when Crabb was seen to be captured. He told him that they saw Crabb in the water, they saw the Russian divers and the ensuing struggle. They made their report but they could not go on record officially for they were precluded from doing so by the Official Secrets Act.

Then there was the case of two Russian seamen on shore leave in Egypt who were approached by a journalist. He was wired with a tape recorder when he entered into conversation with them. He eventually raised the subject of the Crabb case. Both men are reported as having been on board the *Ordzhonikidze* during its visit to

Portsmouth. They knew that a frogman had been captured and taken from the ship by helicopter.

Patricia Rose returned to England where she immediately became embroiled in the Crabb saga, which was constantly being revived in the media by new messages, photographs, meetings and sightings. Whilst waiting to take part in a television programme she was approached by a woman in the studio who had herself just finished a recording. The woman asked casually about Commander Crabb, saying that she had followed the mystery with great interest, and that she could sympathise with Pat's feelings.

The woman then mentioned a photo in *Paris Match* purporting to be Crabb. Pat had not seen this and determined to get hold of a copy.

It was some time later that Pat received a letter from the woman, who was at that time in Rome. It read as follows:

'Via dei Rian
Roma

'I wondered if you'd write and God knows whether I can help at all, or only make matters more bewildering and worrying.

'My memory is bad but when those photographs came out in, was it *Paris Match*, someone, a Czech or a Russian or someone I met here perhaps through Martin Solomon who committed suicide in Spain and who knew Commander Crabb told me that, yes, they knew he was alive and had been told that everyone thought he was dead.

'I think he was working in Vladivostok.

'I'm so sorry not to be able to be more explicit or help you more than to say that since then I've always imagined he was alive.

'I couldn't – alas – hear you speaking much – so maybe you've already said all this and knew this.

'Martin was an extrovert but usually spoke the truth.

'However if I ever hear anymore even via Turkey where I am going to live, I shall write to you at once.

'I shall be here for another month; anything I can do to help I will – funny things crop up in Rome and in Turkey.

'I'm so sorry for you being in love myself with a man in Turkey. I can only imagine what . . .'

The letter is incomplete, and all future contact was made by telephone.

A matter of weeks after the letter reached her, Pat received a telephone call from a man who referred to her meeting and letter from the woman in Italy. From the introduction Pat knew that the caller was genuine so, when he asked if they could meet, she agreed, and a rendezvous was arranged at the Grosvenor Hotel in London, neutral ground for both of them.

The man Pat met gave her some personal details that proved he and his movement had been in touch with Crabb.

'I have been told to inform you that Commander Lionel Crabb is alive, and is an officer serving in the Red Navy. This information has been checked and rechecked to confirm that it is true. I am to say that he will be seeing you again and not to worry.' His final words before he departed were, 'You should make contact with the underground movement called Blok, they have many contacts and they should be able to get quite a lot of information for you.'

This was a totally separate source of information from that to which Bernard Hutton had access.

Pat never received any further letters from the woman but messages that followed referred to her as 'the woman from Turkey'.

These messages then came in the form of apparent chance meetings. Whilst on a train she was confronted by a stranger with a foreign accent who established who she was and told her that Crabb was well and in Russia. She did not believe the man and asked who he was. He declined to identify himself but referred to personal details which were not common knowledge and to which strangers would not have been privy. It confirmed her belief yet again that Crabb was alive.

Three months later, whilst she waited for another train, a different man approached her and asked her to inspect a photograph. She had little time to look at it and it was of poor quality but the man stated that it was Crabb. She was unable to keep the photograph as the man took it back and disappeared.

On 5 January 1962 Soviet naval officer Lieutenant Vadim

Andreyevich defected to the West. He claimed to have served with Commander Lev Lvovich Korablov and was able to provide such precise information and detail that it would appear beyond doubt that Korablov and Crabb were the same person. However, the Admiralty and Government departments still maintained their silence and at no time was any of the evidence acted upon. The British never denied that Crabb had been captured, though, nor did the Russians ever deny having captured him.

Captain Brocklebank, a friend of Pat's, took her to the Polish Club in Kensington where he introduced her to two Polish colonels who were members of the Polish underground movement 'Blok'. They promised to help her to find out as much as possible about her fiancé.

A member of Blok contacted her and said: 'There is definitely no need for you to worry about Commander Lionel Crabb. It is an established fact that he is alive. He holds the rank of Commander in the Red Navy and is in charge of the training of special task divers and frogmen.'

In desperation Pat Rose asked her informers for a letter in Crabb's handwriting, which would prove to her that he was still alive and in Russia. She wrote to the Soviet Premier in an attempt to discover the truth but did not even receive an acknowledgement. Both Britain and Russia were keeping silent over the matter.

The reports through the underground organisation that reached Bernard Hutton followed Crabb – Korablov through his career as a Soviet naval officer. Those bases at which he is reputed to have served are of interest, for they link with bases of the Soviet *Spetsnaz* and Hutton would not have had that information before he died as it was not common knowledge and he never made the link in his writings.

Crabb – Korablov is reported to have served at the Frogman Squadron of the Naval Training Command at Kronstadt. The base is on an island close to Leningrad and is a training centre for Soviet frogmen. It is also a base for the Soviet Naval Infantry which would include a unit of the *Spetsnaz*.

He moved to Arkhangelsk Operational Command which is part of the Northern Fleet, where he would have undergone winter and cold water diving operations. This is a maximum security Soviet base where he could be kept under close surveillance. It would also have restricted any possibility of escape or rescue.

Reports stated that he had a rapid rise in rank and over the years moved to serve in a number of Operational Commands including Odessa on the Black Sea, Sebastopol in the Crimea and Vladivostok in the eastern Soviet Union on the Sea of Japan. All three bases house units of the Naval Infantry and it follows that these would be the centres of naval *Spetsnaz* swimmers and divers. Odessa, mentioned in Chapter 1, is particularly significant for it was the training centre for the *Spetsnaz* swimmer/divers in underwater mine and explosives operations.

If Crabb was sent in by British and American intelligence organisations, and if the reports of his career in the Soviet Navy are accurate, he certainly would have gathered vast amounts of information. On the other hand, if the Soviets had been, through their agents, waiting to capture Crabb and put him to work in their Navy, they would have made good use of his expertise in all Operational Commands.

The reports continue up to 1966, ten years after Crabb's capture and enforced enlistment into the Soviet Navy. By this time he would have been aware that things had gone wrong for nobody had made contact to collect the valuable data. Would the Russians have told Crabb about their infiltration into the British secret service? They would probably have let him assume that he had been dumped because of repercussions at home: the Russians wanted Crabb and the British did not.

What would the Russians do with Crabb – Korablov after his service, for he would have known too much? Reports on Crabb's service state that he was transferred to the Baltic Sea Operation Command to take command of the East German Volksmarine Underwater Unit, where he was in charge of training divers for special tasks at the secret naval base of Boltenhagen, near Lübecker Bay. These East German divers are part of the country's amphibious assault troops and would be used to clear mines and obstructions from possible landing areas in the event of war.

News of Crabb – Korablov, the small stocky diver with a large protruding nose and a strange accent, was reported in the *Ostpreussenblatt*, the newspaper of the East Prussian refugees living in West Germany, which had a vast network of informants in Communist East Germany. It made the statement that Crabb was alive, and reported that he was in Boltenhagen.

The headline was circulated and made headlines in the world's press. Because of the media reaction and the interest in the Crabb affair, Crabb – Korablov was removed from the base and returned to Russia to be kept out of sight. No doubt the authorities were interested in finding out how news of Crabb – Korablov's existence at the base leaked out.

The next report indicates that Crabb – Korablov had been posted back to Sebastopol, to the Red Navy Black Sea Fleet Command, where he became commanding officer of the Special Task Underwater Operational Command which, if true, meant that he was assigned to a *Spetsnaz* operational swimmer/diver unit. Six months after his arrival at this unit, he met Ken Elliott, an Englishman. The year was 1967.

Pat Rose, accompanied by her friend Sylvia, entered the Nag's Head where she had first met Crabb. They found that Len Cole was upstairs in his lounge, not feeling well. Pat ordered a bottle of champagne and glasses for three, and told the barman that they wanted to go up to see Len. He checked that it was all right, and gave them their order.

Pat became aware of a very tall man standing next to her. As she glanced at him, he asked how Mr Cole was keeping, as he was a long-standing friend but he hadn't been in the pub for a long time. Pat explained that he wasn't feeling too good, and that they were going to take him a drink and try to cheer him up. He then took them by surprise by asking if he might join them. Pat saw no objection if Len said it was all right.

Upstairs, the man sat drinking a pint of bitter, whilst the women and Len drank champagne. Len asked how Hutton's book was coming along, and she said that it was ready to be published at any time. He then asked her if a name had been decided upon. She said it had, and that it was to be called *Commander Crabb is Alive*. The man began to laugh, then said to them, 'You don't mean Commander Crabb, you mean Captain Korablov'. Pat was shocked. 'What do you mean? That's the name in a book and it hasn't been published yet.' The man looked round at the company, then said, 'I was with Crabb.'

Pat was flabbergasted and not sure what to do, for she was just about to go on holiday and she wanted Bernard Hutton present if the man was to say anything important, since Hutton had contacts who could corroborate his story. She explained about the holiday, and the man told her not to worry, but to call him when she got back to arrange a meeting. He gave her a business card, providing her with the name Ken Elliott*, and showing that he was a director of Lucas Ltd. The address was an office in Grosvenor Street, London, and had a Mayfair telephone number.

As soon as Pat returned from her holiday she telephoned Hutton and described the meeting at the Nag's Head. She wanted Hutton to be at the next meeting and she gave him the phone number to arrange a time and place. He phoned and spoke to Ken Elliott who agreed to meet the next Thursday at 6.30 pm.

The meeting between Pat Rose, Ken Elliott and Bernard Hutton took place at the Nag's Head, where they found a quiet corner where they could sit and talk without interruption. Ken Elliott made it clear that they should not speak about the meeting nor quote his name for he had to go back to the Soviet Union. Then, looking at Hutton, he asked for his word that the tape with his voice on it should be erased once he had taken the details of the story from it.

The formalities over, Elliott began his story. He described the events that took him on business to the Soviet naval base at Sevastopol. He was accepted by the Russians and had certain freedoms, but always had a state security controller with him, whom he referred to as the 'shadow'. Walking through the base after having conducted some business they went past a ramp where a group of divers were loading equipment from the water into a lorry. The shadow told Elliott, with some pride, that they were from an élite special diving unit. Elliott nodded with approval and replied that they would have to be well trained and need to have good instructors. The shadow stated that they had the best, a unique leader, and indicated a short stocky naval

*Bernard Hutton gave a false name in The Fake Defector to protect Elliott's identity, but owing to subsequent events Pat Rose divulged it to us. It has been established that Ken Elliott did work for Lucas in the overseas service department, and travelled to the USSR. He left the company to live abroad.

officer as the leader. Elliott looked at each of them in turn and told them that is how he first met Captain Korablov or, if calling him by his original name, Commander Crabb.

Pat wanted to know what he looked like. Elliott thought for a moment and described Crabb as wearing the uniform of a Red Navy captain, rather small, about five feet six inches tall, aged in his fifties, with very thick eyebrows, a rather prominent nose and hair on his cheek bones. He explained that it was a face that he would not forget.

Hutton then asked whether Elliott had ever seen a photograph of Crabb prior to the meeting at Sevastopol. Elliott stated that he had only seen photographs of Crabb in the international press, and told them that he had been in the West at the time of his disappearance in 1956. Hutton asked him if he had followed the Crabb affair with any special interest. Elliott confirmed that he had, as he travelled extensively in Russia, and if Crabb had been captured he hoped to meet him. Following on from that, Elliott was asked about his reaction to the headless and handless body that had been found in the sea fourteen months after his disappearance, and which was buried as Crabb in Portsmouth (see next chapter). Elliott replied that he didn't know anything about that event as he had not been in the West at the time, and didn't remember seeing anything about it in the Eastern bloc or Soviet newspapers.

Hutton then produced a photograph and handed it to Elliott. It was an enlarged picture reputedly of First Lieutenant Lev Lvovich Korablov, taken aboard a Soviet naval vessel. Whilst Elliott studied the man depicted in the photograph, Hutton asked if he had ever seen the face before.

After consideration, Elliott stated that the man in the photograph looked like Captain Korablov or Commander Crabb. He had the same eyebrows, nose and mouth, although he looked older now. Hutton moved the conversation back to the meeting in Sevastopol. Elliott described how he and his shadow went to the officers' mess and saw Crabb/Korablov. With the shadow present, Elliott engaged the small man in general conversation. He became certain that the Soviet navy officer he spoke to was Crabb, although he briefly considered the possibility that he could have been a double. The more he spoke the more certain he became that it was Crabb, but he could not challenge the man for the 'shadow' was present and all talk had to be of a general nature.

Pat Rose asked if they spoke in Russian; Elliott said that they did, and that was one reason he was so certain that it was Crabb for the man was certainly not Russian. He paused before continuing to explain that the man spoke Russian fluently but with an unmistakable accent which was certainly not Russian.

Then Elliott came to the important part of the conversation. He told Pat Rose and Bernard Hutton that he was persona grata in the Soviet Union but was kept under constant surveillance, especially at military bases and other sensitive locations. On one particular day, though, Elliott's 'shadow' had been called away leaving the two men alone together. Elliott took the opportunity to ask Korablov point blank whether he was Commander Crabb.

The man did not reply immediately but then asked Elliott if he had to ask awkward questions. The two men sat looking at each other, then Crabb/Korablov looked round to ensure that nobody could overhear them. He asked Elliott if he expected to go to England in the near future. When Elliott confirmed that he did, the man asked if he would contact Pat Rose and pass on a message for him. Elliott agreed. Crabb/Korablov told him that he wanted to put her mind at rest, and told Elliott that he might contact her through the Nag's Head in London, for the landlord Len Cole would know where to find her. Elliott already knew Len Cole, but did not bother to tell Crabb/Korablov this because time was short. Crabb/Korablov told Elliott that, to prove it was really he, he should tell her about the scar on her head, from a car accident, and how her hair grew in a grey streak from the scar, which was why he called her his 'grey witch'. Elliott said that the man then suddenly became tense and stated that he regretted giving the message and that he had been mad to do such a thing.

Pat Rose confirmed that what Elliott had said was correct as only she and Crabbie could link the accident, grey streak and the name 'grey witch'. She had never told anybody, not even Hutton. She was convinced that the message had come from Crabbie.

Wanting to know more she quizzed Elliott as to how Crabb was when they met, and whether he seemed unhappy. Elliott pointed out that it would be virtually impossible for him to escape, and that he was either quite happy or had put on a good façade: he felt from meeting the man that he was happy at doing the job of diving and with the high rank he had reached in the Soviet Navy, but that he did not think kindly about his former country. Elliott then went on to describe Crabb's mannerisms, the way he smoked and coughed, and his gravelly voice. These were details which could be known if he had not met the man – or been briefed very thoroughly.

Hutton then tested Elliott by speaking in Russian, and asking questions about travelling in the Soviet Union. He examined Elliott's passport. Elliott's final statement was to reiterate his concern about the tape for it could compromise both himself and Crabb/Korablov.

As they left Pat Rose asked Elliott if he would be going back to Russia. He told her that he was due to go back soon but that he would be back in England in September: he was going to get married, and told Pat that when they next met he would introduce his new wife to her. It was agreed that Pat should telephone him in September, when he would have tried to get more information about Crabb/Korablov and if possible set up a contact link.

When Pat Rose next saw Len Cole at the Nag's Head, she asked him how long he had known Ken Elliott. He told her that it was some 20 years, but that he did not know much about him, apart from the fact that he was in a business that required him to travel to Russia. He was always well dressed, well mannered and never appeared to be short of money.

Pat waited until September and then telephoned the London office of Lucas and asked to speak to Ken Elliott. The person who answered the telephone told her that Mr Elliott had left the company and was no longer employed by them. Pat was stunned, but she gathered her thoughts and told the woman that Mr Elliott had asked her to contact him in September, after his overseas visit. Could she tell her where she could contact him? The reply was blunt and to the point: Mr Elliott was no longer employed by the company and they had no idea where he was. Pat continued to quiz the woman for Elliott was her only real link with Crabbie, but the woman would make no further comment other than to suggest that she should write to the personnel officer who might be able to help her. This Pat did on a number of occasions, but all her letters to Lucas went unanswered. After 21 years with the company, Ken Elliott had simply disappeared.

In 1968 a Russian merchant navy officer, based in Leningrad, made it known to Bernard Hutton through the underground that he was a close friend of Crabb/Korablov. He explained that he was part of the network that had passed information from Crabb to Pat Rose.

During Hutton's investigations to find out if the officer, Captain R.K. Myelkov, was indeed a friend of Crabb's he explained that they had met whilst on leave in Moscow. The friendship developed over a period of time. Myelkov knew that Crabb/Korablov had been with the East German Volksmarine and that he had been posted back to Sevastopol after the underground had provided the West's news media with details of his work.

Myelkov then offered to provide irrefutable evidence that he was indeed in contact with Crabb, that Crabb was Korablov and that he was alive and in Russia. Hutton was asked to convey this message to Syd Knowles, which he did. Knowles' first reaction was astonishment, but then he became certain it provided strong evidence that Crabbie was alive.

During one meeting I asked Syd the content of the message. He became very edgy and explained that he had never discussed it with anybody before. I could only wait to see if he was prepared to divulge the details. He then told me that it provided strong evidence in the case, so he told me the story, which involved an incident from the war days in Italy. I was stunned also, for it is a story that certainly would not be common knowledge. The details, unfortunately, I cannot repeat for I gave my word to Syd not to publish. Suffice it to say that I understand Syd's reluctance, but also that after careful thought and deliberations we agree that the information must have come from Crabb himself in a desperate bid to make contact with his friends, and let them know he was alive.

With the message delivered, it was agreed that the next time Myelkov was in the West he would meet Syd Knowles and Bernard Hutton to talk about Crabb. On 8 May 1968 Captain Myelkov, master of the 3,246-ton Russian ship *Kolpino*, which was berthed in London docks, prepared to defect. Before he could move to freedom he was found shot dead in his cabin, a shotgun lying near his body.

The following day, the Coroner's Court at Southwark recorded a verdict of suicide. Myelkov was another link in the long chain of the Crabb affair who died at the hands of an unnamed organisation.

Crabb's name was linked with another spy scandal when the British government arrested and charged the Soviet spies Peter and Helen Kroger, who received 20-year prison sentences. The Russians wanted them back as they had valuable information, which was required more urgently as each year passed. The only English person the Russians held was Gerald Brooke, and the British line was that they would never consider exchanging the Krogers for him. The only Soviet option was to try to hold Britain to ransom, and their is some evidence that they did.

It is said that the Soviet Government intended to change Captain Korablov into 'Kapitan Krab' and exhibit him publicly if there was a breakdown in Soviet-British negotiations. The story states that Whitehall maintained its determination not to give in to Soviet pressure. This led to foreign newsmen in Moscow being 'leaked' information about a KGB plan to exhibit Commander Crabb publicly. The *Sunday Express* published a front page despatch from their Moscow correspondent, Mr Roy Blackman, on 22 June 1969.

'CRABB IN MOSCOW SPY SPECTACULAR?

'The fantastic suggestion is being made that the Russians may be planning to present before the world Commander Lionel Crabb, the British frogman spy – named as "Kapitan Krab" of the Soviet Navy. This information came from sources close to the Russian Foreign Ministry in Moscow.'

The *Express* story continued with details of the events in Portsmouth and to report that he had been captured by the Russians and taken to the Soviet Union to serve in their Navy.

Blackman considered that the Russians were testing Britain's reaction and were about to embark on a major propaganda coup. The same sources that released this information predicted in 1967 that the spy Kim Philby was about to make a statement, and he did. Blackman also considered that, if the Russians held Crabb, this could be the

Commander Crabb (left) with Ray Hodges during the resuce attempt on the stricken submarine HMS *Truculent*. (© *Associated Press*)

Crabb with members of his underwater working party in Gibraltar during the war. (© *Imperial War Museum*)

The two photographs of Pat Rose which were printed in an East German newspaper. Only two copies existed, one was held by Pat Rose the other by Crabb. His were never found after his disappearance. (© *Pat Rose*)

The Soviet cruiser *Ordzhonikidze* steams towards Portsmouth in 1956. The bottom of her sister ship, the *Sverdlov*, had been inspected by Crabb and Knowles a few months before Crabb disappeared in Portsmouth harbour. *(© Novosti)*

Soviet frogmen of 1956 wearing one-piece suits with built-in goggles — shows outdated equipment even for that period. The breathing apparatus is heavy and cumbersome. After Crabb's disappearance new and more modern equipment became available. *(© Novosti)*

Mrs Beatrice Crabb, his mother, (facing camera) about to enter the coroner's court. She attended the inquest and funeral but never returned to the grave for she did not believe that her son was buried there. (© *Associated Press*)

Syd Knowles, friend and diving companion for thirteen years, did not attend the funeral and never visited the grave for he knew that it was not the body of Commander Crabb buried there. (© *Unknown*)

Mrs Elaine Crabb with her son after she had left Crabb. Controversy surrounded their relationship, and the time spent away on 'secret' jobs did not help. (© *Pat Rose*)

The photograph produced by Bernard Hutton through his soviet underground contact and said to be that of Commander Crabb, alias First Lt Lev Lvovich Korablov (left) in the Soviet Navy. *(© The estate of Bernard Hutton)*

The whereabouts of Crabb's famous swordstick is unknown , but his medals are in safe hands. L to R . OBE: GM: 39/45 Star: Atlantic Star: Italy Star: Defence Medal: 39/45 Medal. *(© MGW Picture Library)*

We examined old and new photographs of the grave and saw that our recent photo showed a new white stone and different inscription. The headstone had been replaced. (© left, D.Hodgson; right, Welham)

The body of the frogman recovered by the fisherman was similar to that shown. The breathing equipment was not readily available in Britain, but had similarities to the Italian equipment that Crabb preferred to use. (© Imperial War Museum)

A Royal Navy frogman wearing underwater equipment for the 50s . It differed from that found on a dead frogman by a fisherman, before the 'body' washed ashore.
(© Royal Navy)

After Crabb disappeared in 1956, the Soviet Navy embarked upon a programme that was to establish the largest force of combat frogmen in the world. (© Welham)

The Mayeruv Gloriet observation point (where the Czechs made contact with us) overlooking Karlovy Vary and the Imperial Sanatorium. *(© Welham)*

The imposing Imperial Sanatorium at Karlovy Vary. Our Czech contacts told us that it was where Crabb spent his last years. *(© Welham)*

At the Imperial Sanatorium large notices in Czech, Russian, English and German demanded that every visitor must report to the reception. All of the lower level doors and windows were closed and barred. *(© Welham)*

J. Gagarin Colonnade with its five pillars providing a continuous flow of healing waters, photographed at a quiet time. The hall was crowded when contact was made and we were told that Crabb had been in Karlovy Vary. *(© Welham)*

CERTIFIED COPY OF AN ENTRY OF DEATH

GIVEN AT THE GENERAL REGISTER OFFICE, LONDON

Application Number B36086

REGISTRATION DISTRICT Chichester

1957. DEATH in the sub-district of Chichester North in the County of West Sussex

Columns:—	1	2	3	4	5	6	7	8	9
No.	When and Where died	Name and surname	Sex	Age	Occupation	Cause of death	Signature, description and residence of informant	When registered	Signature of registrar
259	Tenth June 1957 in Chichester Harbour Sx.	Lionel Kenneth Philip CRABB	Male	48 pars	1st Hans Road London S.W.3. Retired Commander Royal Naval Volunteer Reserve	Not ascertainable P.M.	Certificate Received from E.L. Brickman coroner for West Sussex (England?) after inquest held 26th November 1957	Twenty ninth June 1957	[signature] Registrar

CERTIFIED to be a true copy of an entry in the certified copy of a Register of Deaths in the District above mentioned.
Given at the GENERAL REGISTER OFFICE, LONDON, under the Seal of the said Office, the 26th day of September 1986

This certificate is issued in pursuance of the Births and Death Registration Act 1953. Section 34 provides that any certified copy of an entry purporting to be sealed or stamped with the seal of the General Register Office shall be received as evidence of the birth or death to which it relates without any further or other proof of the entry, and no certified copy purporting to have been given in the said Office shall be of any force or effect unless it is sealed or stamped as aforesaid.

CAUTION:—It is an offence to falsify a certificate or to make or knowingly use a false certificate or a copy of a false certificate intending it to be accepted as genuine to the prejudice of any person, or to possess a certificate knowing it to be false without lawful authority.

DX 360405

From A504M Dd 8923988 50m 3/86 Mcr(931735)

Crabb's death certificate.

time to produce him – when the negotiations over a swap between Gerald Brooke and the Russian super-spies, the Krogers, were getting nowhere.

The Foreign Office were asked for their view on the statements, and responded that they never commented 'on stories of this kind'. Mr Blackman's story was corroborated by other press correspondents.

On 2 June 1969 the Foreign Office categorically denied that there was any question of an exchange of the Krogers for Brooke.

On 24 July 1969 Gerald Brooke was released and flown home from Moscow: he had served four years of his five-year sentence for distributing anti-Soviet leaflets. Russia's spies, Peter and Helen Kroger, who had served only eight years of their sentences, were granted freedom on 24 October 1969.

The exposure of Crabb did not materialise and the naval diver's name was dropped from the world's press yet again. Crabb – Korablov, who was reported to have been removed from the Sevastopol operational command, now returned to continue his service.

8

The Body

Mr John Randall was out fishing in Chichester Harbour with two friends, Ted and Bill Gilby, on Sunday 9 June 1957, when they spotted something floating in the water. At first they thought that it was an old tractor tyre but not being certain decided to recover it. With great difficulty they managed to haul it into the boat, where they found it to be a body, dressed in a black rubber suit. The suit had marine growth on it indicating that it had been in the water for some time. The corpse had neither head nor hands. It was just 14 months since Commander Crabb disappeared in Portsmouth. They took the corpse to Pilsea Island and reported it to the Royal Air Force station at Thorney Island. Mr Randall then returned to the boat to await the arrival of the police who made arrangements for the body to be moved to Chichester mortuary.

Upon its arrival, a report states, the mortuary keeper was told not to carry out his normal procedure of preparing the body for its post-mortem examination. On 10 June 1957 it was Dr Donald Plimsoll King, a pathologist, who examined the remains of a male body clothed in a frogman's suit. A tight band fitted around the middle of the suit, leaving the upper torso a collection of bones and fragments of flesh. The skull and hands were missing. The lower part of the body was well preserved and he found no recognisable scars or injuries, nor did the radiological report indicate 'any evidence of bone injury'. Four features were submitted for use in possible identification.

1. Length of feet 22.2cms (8.75 inches).
2. Moderate degree of bilateral hallux valgus (the big toe was turned out).

3. He was uncircumcised.
4. The pubic hair was light brown in colour.

It was not possible to determine the cause of death and Dr King could only offer limited information for possible identification.

The rubber diving suit was in good condition apart from being covered in marine growth, except for a number of places around the legs, described by Detective Superintendent Alan Hoare, in charge of the enquiry, as 'marks of rust', making it seem 'apparent that the body had been held by being caught on an underwater metal object'. Perhaps, we may conjecture, something had been attached to the body to hold it underwater. There were no identification marks or serial numbers visible on the suit, which is not surprising as it was not Royal Navy issue. It was based on the Italian diving suits and designed and manufactured by Heinke of London. As described earlier, this differed in design from the British suit which was one-piece, whereas this suit consisted of two pieces joined in the middle. To keep the two parts of the suit together and maintain a seal, a rubber cummerbund was worn. Dr King stated that it was this band which had halted decomposition of the lower part of the body.

In the attempt to make an identification the authorities called upon a selected number of people. Mrs Margaret Elaine Crabb was taken to the mortuary at Bognor Regis on 11 June 1957. She entered the building and was shown a body. In the statement she made to the inquest, she said that she could not identify the feet as being those of her former husband. However, Syd Knowles and the other naval officer both state that she did not see the body.

One person who did was Sydney Knowles, BEM, Crabb's diving companion for 13 years. He was the ideal witness for, as he told us, 'over the years of diving it was only natural that I had seen the Commander in a state of undress, So I can say that, yes, I would know his body.' The authorities were aware of this and dispatched members of the Preston CID to interview him in order to obtain accurate details of any marks or deformities that Crabb had. Syd was called to identify the body and described on a tape recording, in the presence of Pat Rose, the events of that visit, and confirmed to us that the contents were correct in every detail.

'Two days after Commander Crabb's body being found I was visited at the swimming pool where I then was by two people. They were tall chaps in civilian clothing, bowler hatted, etc., who introduced themselves as a colonel and captain. They said they were members of some intelligence organisation, but not naval intelligence, MI5 I think. They asked whether I would go and see the remains of a body at Chichester, a body in a rubber suit, since I might be able to give the answer as to whether it was Commander Crabb. They said, "We believe you have been in touch with CID Preston and they have taken a statement from you, referring to identification marks." I said I had and they wanted to know how long I had known him, the colour of his hair and so on.'

Syd continued: 'I motored down to Chichester, but before going down I was called to Fleet Street and asked by the *Daily Mirror* if I would give them any information, or could they build a story around my visit to Chichester. For this they would pay me £45, and £45 was £45 then. I wasn't going to tell them anything people didn't know, that was as far as I was concerned – I was told to meet their reporter in Chichester.

'About ten miles outside Chichester I was stopped by a police car, and the two men who had come to see me at the swimming pool, the MI5 people. There was another car there, and they asked me to get into it. They said, "We would like to talk to you prior to you going down to see the body." I said, "Why stop me here?" He said, "This, as you know, Mr Knowles, is a very dodgy business, embarrassing to the country and to Commander Crabb." I replied, "It is embarrassing to the country." I wasn't awfully in love with the Russians, I didn't hate them, I wasn't awfully in love with them, so I said "yes", I would help them in any possible way.

'They then told me, "When you see the body – when you go into Chichester, you will go into the mortuary. I want you first of all to see the Chief Inspector. He will have a word with you – you will go along with him and go into the mortuary and they will show you the body. You will then tell him the reasons why you know the person who the body is. I said "Very well, is this the only reason you stopped me going straight in, like?" and he said, "Well, we don't want you speaking to any reporters." "Oh! Just a minute," I said. "If I don't

[91]

I'm going to lose some money here. I've been offered £45 to give a good story after this Chichester visit to the *Daily Mirror*." He said, "Well, I'm afraid you'll have to be very careful what you say to them, in other words you say this" – and he carried on to say what I could tell them and what I couldn't tell them.

'He then said, "While you were in the Navy you signed the Official Secrets Act." I told him that I signed it twice, but that was well over ten years ago. He said, "Here's another document we would like you to sign." It had Official Secrets Act written on the top, there was small print, on four or five sheets of paper, and I signed three out of the four or five sheets at the bottom. It was not the same form that I signed in the Navy appertaining to the Official Secrets Act, it was certainly not the same form. Now I'm wondering if or not this form was the genuine thing. This I don't know – possibly it was, it might have been a revised form. I signed it in the car and he put the document in the briefcase. He said, "Well, now, you go ahead in the normal way." I went and reported to the Inspector. He took me to the mortuary in a car, not my car, in a police car. He took me into a building where the remains were laid out.

'I identified the body – no! I looked at the body – the scars that I'd described and sketched on the form were not in absolutely the same place as I knew them, either in shape or place. I said, "This is not the body of Commander Crabb. Commander Crabb's hair was sandy – the body hair . . ." ' Pat interrupted at this point, 'His hair was black.'

Syd replied, 'I wouldn't call it black – his body hair was sandy and this person's was absolutely jet black. What you'd expect to come from either Greek or Italian style of colouring, not the skin, the hair was so dark that it must have been a Latin. I said, "No, this is not the body of Commander Crabb." I said, "The scars are very much like them and they are almost in the same position but there is one missing, the inverted Y on the back of his leg, the back of his calf." I said, "No. This is not the body of Commander Crabb." Oh!, prior to seeing the body there was a chap in civilian clothes in there, a chap in a white coat, a long white coat, and another chap in a white coat. The civilian asked these two people to leave prior to me looking at the body.

'He said, "Are you absolutely sure this is not Commander Crabb?" I said I was as sure as I could be considering the state of the body. The legs, for instance, were like parchment, all the skin was virtually white. I had to stretch the skin to search for the scars. It was mummified, virtually mummified and the skin was snow-white. Have you seen a lump of fat off a carcass? – it was like that, snow-white. Also, the lower part of the body, on the back of the thighs and back of the knees around the lower part of the legs, not quite near the ankles, was badly marked. It looked as if something had been biting them.

'I thought that if the body had been held under the water by chain or cable, or even caught up in some wreckage, that's the sort of identification there would be in the skin. I said, "This is not the body of Commander Crabb; as far as I can ascertain this is not the body of Commander Crabb."

'He said, "Very well. This gentleman would like to say a few words to you." He then left the room. With the body between us this chap said to me, "Mr Knowles, we know this is not the body of Commander Crabb, but I want you to say that it is the body of Commander Crabb." I said, "Well, why should I say that?" He said, "Commander Crabb was a great patriot. He loved his Queen and Country, and so we ask that you don't embarrass the country and don't embarrass him." He said, "If he could speak to you here, he'd say please don't embarrass the Queen and Country." I said, "He would, actually, indeed he would." He said, "Will you go with me on this and sign the documents?" I said, "What, the Official Secrets Act?" then added, "I don't know any secrets." He said, "Well, this is a secret. When you go in court and you're asked, did you identify the body, will you please say, that is the body of Commander Crabb?" I said, "Yes, I will," and I really meant it, I really believed about this embarrassment to the country and I know that Crabbie would have wanted me to say that.'

Pat said, 'You don't believe that was Crabbie, do you?'

'I don't,' responded Syd.

'That's what he said to me on the train, I love you but my Queen and my country come first,' said Pat.

Syd continued with his story. 'Just prior to going out, before he

[93]

called those people back in the room, he said to me, "Don't forget, if you are asked in court by Commander Crabb's solicitor or by the coroner or anyone else, do you swear to me that you will try to convince them that it is Commander Crabb's body?" I said, "Very well, I'll do that." '

On Tuesday 11 June, at Chichester Magistrate's Court, Mr Bridgman opened the inquest. The only evidence submitted was the detailed list of equipment found on the body, which comprised 1 frogman's two-piece suit, 1 pair swim fins, 2 sorbo pads, 1 pair bathing trunks, 1 pair nylon socks, 1 pair blue combinations (top missing), 1 pair nylon combinations and 1 piece of an undervest. The proceedings were adjourned.

The Admiralty had sent Lieutenant W. Y. McLanachan from HMS *Vernon* to assist with identification of the body, the rubber suit, flippers, and underclothes. What constructive evidence could be obtained from an officer who had not actually dived with Crabb is a mystery. He only stated that he saw a frogman's rubber two-piece suit, swim fins which were similar to Royal Naval issue type and an assortment of undergarments. He could not say that they belonged to Crabb, nor could he definitely identify the body.

It was not apparent that the identification of the body found off Chichester rested on the undergarments reputed to have been removed from the body. We have seen that the mortuary keeper did not prepare the body as he would normally have done. Mr Bridgman said that it might be some time before he issued a certificate for the burial of the body, as he would not issue one while identification remained possible. The reason for the delay (when one knows the evidence provided by Sydney Knowles) is an unknown factor, apart from the fact that it provided time to prepare for the final inquest which the authorities wanted to pass without problems.

On Wednesday 26 June 1957, the inquest was resumed. Dr King was called to give evidence of his findings from the post-mortem examination.

On 10 June 1957 he made an examination of some human remains at Chichester Public Mortuary and when he saw them they were clothed in a frogman's suit. Above the waist, parts of the body including the skull had disappeared although certain bones, including the left humerus and both scapulae, remained. The abdominal cavity was empty except below the waist-band of the suit. The organs had undergone extensive post-mortem change including a change known as adipocere, but they were recognisable. He identified a photograph as being one of the remains and said that another was an actual size photograph of the feet. He had found the measurement of the feet to be 8.75 inches which was small for an adult man. He also found that there was a condition called hallux valgus which was a condition of the toes in which the big toe, which was the hallux, was turned outwards. The joint of the big toe was enlarged and disjointed. With regard to the hair on the body, the pubic hair was intact and the colour was clearly a light brown and in certain lights when dry it had a gingerish tinge. He thought the deceased was rather a small man in the region of 5' 6". The legs were in a good state of preservation and he would describe them as being muscular and well formed, and, apart from the feet, there was no deformity. They were quite straight.

From the adipocere, he concluded that the body had been in the water for at least six months and could well have been in the water for fourteen months or more.

On 14 June 1957, Dr King went to the mortuary and examined the remains again. On this occasion he reported a scar, 'left side left knee – inverted Y? A photograph* was taken at Chichester Police Station in his presence of the portion of the skin bearing this scar.

Why did the coroner not question the fact that in Dr King's original report there was *no* mention of any scars on the lower part of the body, when in fact two vital marks for possible identification were on Crabb's body? Did Knowles' drawings of the scars' locations have any bearing on this change in the statement? In other words, was a scar which had not been there previously 'created' to try to conform to what Syd Knowles had said? Or was Dr King intimidated into adding material to his testimony?

Mrs Margaret Elaine Crabb gave evidence about her marriage and divorce. She continued to say that during the short time of their married life he was serving in the Royal Naval Volunteer Reserve and shortly

*Photographs taken for an inquest are kept with the statements and coroner's report, but in this case the photographs of the body and scars were removed from the records.

after they were married he became a commander. She described him as a short man and said that he was not as tall as she, her height being 5′ 5″. His legs were very straight and muscular and the hair on his body was very light brown inclined to ginger. His feet were small and his big toes were very unusual. They appeared to be what she thought were hammer toes and were raised high of the ground. The photograph of the body's feet were shown to her, and she said that they were *not* as she remembered them. She thought he took a size 6 shoe. She continued that on 11 June 1957 she went to the Bognor mortuary and there saw the remains of a human body. She could not identify the feet as those of her former husband although she was not able to say definitely that they were not his feet.

It is recorded that Mrs Crabb could not say whether or not her husband had been circumcised 'as sexual relations were not normal'. 'It was because of his abnormal sexual behaviour that I divorced him,' she told the Chichester police.

John Randall provided evidence of the find and stated that on 9 June 1957 he was out in his fishing boat accompanied by two men by the name of Gilby. He went down the harbour from Bosham until he got to a point where he saw a black object floating in the water about 30 yards from the boat just surfacing with the little running tide showing just above the water every few seconds. They circled the object on several occasions and he decided it was not a buoy or a small mine as he thought at first and, upon closer examination, it appeared to be a tractor tyre because there were two large ribs showing just above the water. He was not satisfied and so went alongside the object and pulled it aboard with a boat hook. He then immediately saw it was the shape of a body and on examination he formed the opinion that it contained the body of a person in a rubber diving suit. The ridges he had seen were the two waist-band ridges. They towed the body in to Pilsea Island and then reported it to the Royal Air Force Station at Thorney Island. He then returned and waited for the arrival of the police.

Police Constable Ronald G. Williams, stationed at Southbourne, stated that at about 12 noon on 9 June 1957 he went to the Royal Air Force Station at Thorney Island and accompanied the Station medical officer to Pilsea Island. On the beach he saw some human remains. They were part of the body of a man dressed in a rubber frogman's suit. The head and upper portion of the body and the arms were missing.

Detective Superintendent Alan Hoare of the West Sussex Constabulary said that he had been in charge of enquiries in connection with the body which was found in Chichester harbour on the 9 June 1957. He made enquiries from all the police forces on the south coast from Cornwall to Kent and from those enquiries he had been informed that *no* other person similarly dressed to the body recovered had been reported missing. On 23 October 1955 there was a man reported missing after diving in the River Dart, but his clothing was in no way similar to the clothing in this case.

Why, one wonders, did Detective Superintendent Hoare make no mention of the body found earlier by Harry Cole? As will be seen later in the book, Cole's evidence would have been of vital importance.

Miss Amy Thomas also gave evidence. She was the manageress of a number of service flatlets at 2a Hans Road, London. A gentleman named Commander Crabb occupied one of these for some five years off and on for periods until April 1956. While at that address he was working for some furniture people, but she had no idea in what capacity. Early in April 1956, he told her he was going to be away for a few days on business and a few days after that, on Tuesday 17 April 1956, he told her he was just leaving. He never came back.

One person whose evidence was interesting was the Managing Director of Heinke and Co Ltd of Bermondsey, London. Mr Eric James Blake stated that his firm manufactured, among other things, underwater swim suits. He knew Commander Crabb. On three occasions his company had supplied Crabb with underwater suits, the last one being on 11 October 1955; this suit was unusual in that it had a neck seal and did not have a hood, for normally such suits were sold with hoods. He had seen the suit found on the deceased and said that this was designed in about January 1955. During the ten months between the time it was designed and the time a suit was sold to Commander Crabb in October 1955 they sold about fifteen suits identical in all respects to that found on the deceased. The suit he had seen at Chichester Police Station was identical to the one sold to Crabb but he was unable to say, of course, whether it was the same

[97]

suit. Thus, if a cover-up had been undertaken, other suits were available.

Apart from the very limited evidence provided by Lieutenant McLanachan, the only other person representing the Admiralty was George William Bostock, a temporary clerical officer in the Department of the Admiral Commanding Reserves, at Queen Anne's Mansions, London SW1. He said that it was part of his duty to keep records of Royal Naval Volunteer officers. One of the files under his control related to Commander Lionel Kenneth Philip Crabb and this record showed that he was born on 28 January 1909. He entered the Navy and on 30 April 1948 he was released with the rank of Temporary Acting Lieutenant Commander. He was recalled to active service on 12 October 1951 with the substantive rank of Lieutenant Commander and on 30 June 1952 he was promoted to the rank of Commander. On 8 April 1955 he was finally released from active service and since that date he had not at all been employed in the service of the Navy or done any training.

As the court was dealing with a body and not the career of Commander Crabb, why were his naval medical records not requested? They would have given valuable information in the identification of the body, especially since they would have contained details of any feet abnormalities.

Sydney Knowles gave straightforward evidence to the coroner. He was at present a swimming pool supervisor. He had joined the Royal Navy in December 1939 and he first met Commander Crabb in 1941 when he did underwater work with him. In the winter of 1945, they were serving at Leghorn and the captains of the ships had been instructed to have rolls of barbed wire place below the water marks of their ships for protection against Italian frogmen. Early one morning Commander Crabb and he were going below the surface to search for limpet mines and they were going to investigate the American ship *John Harrison* to see that mines were not present. As they were going down, a tug came along casting up a wash which threw both of them against the barbed wire of this ship. When they went back to their launch, Knowles noticed that Commander Crabb had sustained a wound on the side of his left knee. He dressed it for him. About three weeks later, when he was working with Crabb again, he noticed a

THE BODY

scar – it was in the shape of an inverted 'Y'. This was the scar Dr
King reported after his second examination of the body. However,
in his statement to the police, Syd had also reported a second scar,
roughly the size of an old sixpence, on Crabb's right thigh, which
had been caused by a seawater boil. This evidence was not produced
at the inquest.

Syd's testimony also said that after the war he saw Crabb from time
to time and knew that he was living at 2a Hans Road, London. He
was also quite familiar with the clothing that he wore when diving.
He wore a two-piece rubber suit with a neck seal instead of a hood.
He used to wear a pair of maroon swimming shorts and he had two
sets of combination underwear to wear alternately, one khaki in colour
and the other blue. He also used to wear blue socks. Syd was not
able to say from the photograph shown to him whether the feet were
those of Crabb.

Apart from the second scar which was *not* recorded by the pathologist,
Syd also stated that Crabb had been trying out diving suits
manufactured by Heinke's of London. When they were together on
a diving job at Tobermory, he was wearing Italian Tenth Flotilla MASS
fins and a Heinke two-piece diving suit. '*He never wore British fins.
He hated them,*' Syd told the police. 'He damaged his fins in 1954
at Tobermory and I loaned him my Italian fins. When I last saw him
in the "Captain's Cabin", I said to him: "When are you going to
return my fins?" and he said: "I can't at the moment. I shall require
them, but I will let you have a pair when I go to Italy on business
re the book and visit the Italian frogmens' headquarters." '

The Italian fins are the same as ordinary fins, but much lighter than
the British naval type. The left fin is marked 'Sinistro' and the right
one is marked 'Destro'. The fins on the body which was recovered
were of the British naval issue type, so why was this evidence not
raised? The Italian fins belonging to Syd were never found amongst
Crabb's belongings after his disappearance, and it is evident that he
would not wear British fins if he had Italian ones available.

Syd also said in that statement that Commander Crabb did not have
hammer toes. His feet were quite normal and in healthy condition.

The coroner recorded an open verdict as it was impossible to
determine the cause of death. Based upon the evidence provided, the

feet, the scar, the colour of hair and the rubber suit, he determined that the body found in Chichester harbour was that of Commander Crabb. The death certificate issued on 28 June 1957 stated the cause of death to be 'NOT ASCERTAINABLE. P.M.'

On Friday 5 July 1957, the body of the unknown man was buried at Milton Cemetery, Portsmouth. There were no official representatives of the Royal Navy at the funeral, and neither Sydney Knowles or Pat Rose attended. Mrs Beatrice Crabb, Crabb's mother, attended, but did not in her heart believe that it was the grave of her son.

Sydney Knowles recalls that, at a meeting after the burial with Pat Rose and Bernard Hutton, he said that: 'In court I felt that everyone had been primed, the right questions were never asked, and the obvious questions were never asked. People that they asked certain questions to were people that as far as I knew didn't know that much about Crabb, and they asked people the questions that couldn't give the answers.'

Bernard Hutton asked, 'You surely know that Crabbie had what they call hammer toes, don't you?' 'No. Crabbie's big toe was a broad toe, a hammer toe is a toe that turns over the top of the other one. This wasn't Crabb's body, I know that.' Hutton responded, 'Crabb's former wife said she did not think it was the body of her husband because he had hammer toes and this body did not.'

Knowles was emphatic: 'It was not Crabb's body, and they told me that themselves.'

Hutton asked Syd what his first reaction had been when he read in the papers that a body had been found which was thought to be Crabbie's. Syd said, 'I felt there was no way that it could be. I said he was too experienced to have been killed in the water. He would have managed to hide, a layman would not realise how easy it was for a diver to disappear if he wanted to. With the tides he could have lost himself in two minutes.'

If the body buried in Milton Cemetery was not that of Commander Crabb, then whose was it?

Mrs Beatrice Crabb, Commander Crabb's mother, had not been called to the inquest or asked to provide any information regarding he son. She attended the funeral which was without full military honours and the headstone placed on the grave was engraved: 'In Ever

Loving Memory of My Son Commander Crabb. At Rest At Last.'
There were no Christian names, no date and no mention of his
decorations, a strange epitaph under any normal circumstances, but
then the circumstances were not normal.

Mrs Crabb stated, 'They say it was the body of my son, and so
I suppose I must believe them.' However, in later years, before she
died, she confided in friends, 'My son Lionel is not buried there.'
After the funeral she never again visited the grave.

We have seen that Sydney Knowles emphatically denied that the
body was Commander Crabb's, for very sound reasons; moreover he
was told in the mortuary that the body was not that of Commander
Crabb. Syd told me, 'The Commander and I went through a lot
together both during and after the war, we saved each other's lives
more than once, and I would have followed him on a job anywhere.
Do you think that if I believed that the grave in Portsmouth was his
that I'd not have been back to it and indeed attended the funeral?
I don't know who they buried but it wasn't Crabbie, no way.'

Pat Rose declared, 'That's not Crabbie buried at Milton, my dear,
if it was I would have been back.' She paused before continuing, 'I
wasn't in England when they buried the body, so I didn't go to the
funeral, and even if I had been here, I wouldn't have gone. It wasn't
Crabbie, and they [the authorities] have as good as admitted it.'

'Whose body do you think it is?'

'I don't know, some poor nobody who was taken from some morgue,
and placed in that place to look like Crabbie.'

'Do you think it was the Russians as Hutton described in his book?'
I asked.

She paused, then said, 'No, I believe that it was MI5 or whatever
department does that sort of thing. It's the way they seem to do things.'

'Then what about the woman who puts the flowers on the grave?'
I enquired.

'That's probably the poor mother or wife, whose relation is buried
there,' she responded. 'It's not Crabbie,' she continued in a low voice.
'I spoke to Mrs Crabb, his mother, and she told me that it was not
her Lionel. That's cruel, when a mother doesn't know whether her
son is alive or dead.'

I continued, 'I'm not sure where the body came from, the Russians or our people, but have you visited the grave?'

'Once out of curiosity, but never as the grave of Crabbie.'

Bernard Hutton relates in his book that Crabb was captured in Portsmouth, taken to Russia, and forced to serve in the Soviet Navy. He suggests that as a precaution the Russians found a body similar in status to Crabb's, removed the head and both hands, and dressed it in Crabb's undergarments and rubber suit. To eliminate any other possibility of identification the body was placed under controlled conditions in the sea, and held by cables around the legs and thighs to decompose.

Months later, because of developments in the media and reports of Crabb being in Russia it was decided to deposit the body on a British beach, where it would be presumed to be that of Crabb. Hutton's theory reasoned that the British Government would not deny that it was Crabb's and that they would wish to act quickly in the matter of identification and disposal.

Hutton claimed that the Russians decided to activate the plan and had the body removed from its original location in the sea. Three submarines moved down the English Channel on their way to the Indian Ocean, and Hutton describes – from evidence (?) he obtained from a secret Soviet dossier – how one of the submarines towed a sealed container, inside which was the body. At a location where the currents seemed ideal to carry it to the coast, the body was released to float away. The submarines continued on their journey down the Channel. Three days later the body was found by John Randall. Hutton and the media raised the question of the submarines' passage, but the authorities never followed it up, either at the inquest or subsequently.

9

Crabb Korablov

Crabbie was born into a comfortably-off middle class family, recalled Pat Rose. 'He was an only child and his father was killed during the First World War, when he was only five years old. His mother never re-married.

'In his younger days, his playmates were his cousins and he used to go on holidays to Eastbourne where they stayed at the Grand Hotel. He told me that the best part of those holidays was when the man in the lift let him control it, and he spent time going up and down.

'He went to Brighton college but did not get on very well and he referred to himself as the "black sheep of the family" in so far as he was an adventurer whilst his cousins followed the more orthodox professions. His ambition was to go to sea, and at one time a merchant navy cadet, but an eyesight defect – he called it "a lazy eye" – changed all of his plans.

'When he was in his early twenties, he came into a substantial inheritance and decided to travel around the world. He took two years about it, travelling in tramp steamers, staying wherever he fancied. He went through most of his money, both spending and lending, for he was never slow to help others.

'Back in Britain, he ran an advertising business in Adelphi, then sold it to a commercial artist who had worked for him. His luck changed yet again and he inherited more money and decided to go and live in China. One wet night, four friends gave themselves hangovers seeing him off in a tramp steamer, from London docks. He was away for a year, living with a Chinese family. Before he left, the man with whom he lived, and had taught him Chinese, gave him a piece of jade as a present.

'Crabbie always wore it round his neck,' said Pat. 'Later, when in England, somebody repaid a loan that he had made them, but the cheque was bad. Poor old Crabbie was broke, and he had to sell his jade talisman. The dealer gave him only £7.

'He told me of the banquets that would last for days,' recalled Pat. 'He was a small eater so he suffered. He also had a strange thing, his jaw would click when he ate, and that caused him great embarrassment.

'Crabbie had a crush on me long before we really met but of course I did not know it, and anyway I was in love with Peter Aitken. When dear Crabbie and I did eventually get together, he was a darling, and he loved me so much. He was good fun to be with and at the time I suppose that was enough for me, but he was more serious than I was. We lived near each other in London and so met a lot. He was always the gentleman and really enjoyed going out. We would enter a club or restaurant as if we owned the world, we were happy together.

'I remember once, when Crabbie was on board the Navy's diving ship . . .' she paused, thinking, 'what was its name? Oh, yes, *Reclaim* – was there a ship called *Reclaim*?'

'Yes, it was the Navy's deep-diving ship, HMS *Reclaim*.'

'Right, HMS *Reclaim*. Well, he invited me aboard to dinner. It was lovely, I was treated like a queen, and I had really dressed up in nice clothes, for Crabbie liked to see me well dressed – he always looked smart himself,' she paused, 'except when he was diving, but that's different isn't it? Anyway, on the ship, Crabbie was proud of me and we had a wonderful time. I can remember, we had some difficulty getting down the gangway afterwards.

'It was after we were engaged the first time that he had to go away, and I don't know what really happened but we drifted apart. That hurt Crabbie really deeply and as a result I went to France and married Ian Rose. Crabbie married, but it only lasted a short time, he was not for her, as he told me later, I was the only one, and I agreed that we were well suited, for neither was happy in love. It's so difficult to explain. Whilst I was still in France, Crabbie telephoned me. He sounded as if he had to speak to someone, and chose me. He said he had been on a job which involved him looking at a Russian ship and that the Russians were after him. I have since heard that he was taken to Russia by submarine and he dived from it to have a look under a ship. I think he was lucky to get away with it. That happened in 1952 or 1953. I can't remember exactly.

'I contacted Crabbie when I was going to leave France and he arranged accommodation for me, and looked after everything when I arrived. We were together again, just like the old times, and we were soon seen together by our old friends. It was a wonderful period, and I hoped that things may have worked out better this time, both having had such dreadful experiences.

'I remember having to go to court for my divorce, which was granted. Crabbie was elated and took me and my lawyer out for champagne, and he said to the barrister, "It's a good thing you're not one of my men, look at your tatty old robe" – such was Crabbie! He wanted to marry me straight away, but I said that we must gather ourselves first, then we could think of marriage.

'I think Crabbie had left the Navy. I never saw him in uniform, but he would pop off to Portsmouth and after a few days return, and carry on as if nothing had happened.

'You know of course that he joined up with Pendock, whom he had known for a long time. He had a business selling cocktail bar furniture or something like that. Anyway, Crabbie joined him and began going around selling the furniture. From what I knew of it, it seemed to be doing quite well, but he still disappeared for odd times. He used to tell people, friends that is, that he was settling down and doing well in the furniture job for me, he was a darling, but he was always telling me – "Pat, I would do anything for you but remember, my Queen and Country come first." Do you know, he really meant it, he loved his country and his monarch above all else.'

'He undertook a dive under the *Sverdlov* in October the previous year,' I said. 'How did he react before that job?'

'As I said, he would often go away and that one was no different, I recall him saying that he was off to do a little job for the Admiralty and that he would be diving with Syd again, and that pleased him because they were great friends, in fact Crabbie loved Syd and I do mean that in the deep meaning of friendship, because Crabbie was not a homosexual. You do understand that, don't you, because I know it has been said before, and I absolutely refute that.' Pat was adamant about that.

'Anyway, Crabbie and Syd went and did the job. I don't know what they found, but they seemed pleased.

'On the last job, when he went to look at the – I can't pronounce the name . . .'

'The *Ordzhonikidze*,' I said.

'Yes, that's right, well he was not himself. He wanted Syd to go with him, but poor Syd could not. I told Crabbie not to go, you see, there was far more to the job than having a quick look under some ship, poor old Crabbie was desperately concerned about whatever it was he had to do.'

Pat paused and thought. 'You know, he made more of the coming back than he ever had before, when we were going to Portsmouth. I had to call in to the flats where I lived to tell the lady who looked after them, and Crabbie looked at some metal objects, I can't remember what they were, but he asked the woman what she was going to do with them. She told him that they were awaiting the rubbish collectors. He then asked if he could have them, and she was pleased that somebody was going to take them away. Crabbie told her he would pick them up in a couple of days. I don't know what he wanted the things for.'

'So he wasn't acting his normal self?'

'No, that's why I was so concerned when he did not return to London. I knew it was more involved than "just a little dip", as he called it.

'Crabbie was a character and it was inevitable that he associated with like minds, and one dear friend with whom he shared a flat in London contacted me.'

On 27 January 1969, from his home in Gibraltar, Noel 'Skeffy' Fitzpatrick wrote to Pat . . .

'Dear Pat,

'Do you remember meeting me – many long years ago – in "The Gate House" at the corner of Ennismore Mews, Kensington (or was it Knightsbridge?) – when and where I came to realise how fond of one another you and (my very dear friend) "Crabbie" had become. All the enclosed is self-explanatory; but there is nothing that your or I can do in the matter . . . short of an exhumation of the mortal remains found in a rubber diving suit drifting in Chichester harbour. It would seem that we have everybody against us! Can we prevail? Please favour me with your views. Did you see the film that those ignorant people made about him? Laurence Harvey did his best; but the director knew absobloody-lutely nothing about that singularly courageous, lovable and gallant chivalrous MAN whom you and I know and knew. Furthermore, WHERE is the sword-stick, which I gave him? The rather over-large knob of oxidised silver was engraved (to my design) with a golden crab! I was told that his friend Penrose [sic] has possessed himself of "Crabbie's" lucky talisman. It should, of course, have been offered to me for "safe-keeping" pending the return (if possible) of Crabbie himself. As I am still something of a nomad – it is my desire that permission be obtained from "Their Lordships" (of the Admiralty) to have this well-known memento of a brave naval officer placed on display in the Royal Navy Museum. May I count upon your support in all that I have written above? Do please try to find time during which to get in touch with me and let us see what together we can do!

'Yours ever sincerely,
(signed) Noel "Skeffy" Fitzpatrick.'

Pat responded at once, assuring him that she would help in any way possible as she sought details of her Crabbie's fate.

Fitzpatrick's second letter to Pat, dated 19 February 1969, provides another insight into the Commander who just disappeared.

'Most splendid Pat,
'Your inspiring letter dated a mere two days ago has just reached me, and I make haste to reply.

'I am quite thrilled to bits to learn about my wonderful heroic little friend. Long ago have I forgiven him for smashing up my 4½-litre "Invicta" 4-door saloon, with me and "Bill" Nangle in the back of the vehicle. It was a wet old road and could have caused disaster to a bishop – so it could!! That must have been in the summer of 1938

[107]

and not only was the car wrecked but also Eastern Command manoeuvres to which we added to realism the bringing down of a telegraph pole. When you and the "Admiral" get together again, I only hope the riot-police and the Fire Brigade do not need to have to go into action. Dear Pat, how can I express my profound appreciation of your determined efforts towards restoring liberty to this grand little man – so courageous and the very symbolism of that "two-o'clock in the morning" courage – which I myself have never possessed!

'Nothing less than thirty well-armed soldiers behind me with their rifles and bayonets would have sufficed to give me the courage to win the medals which I did. Compared to Crabbie, I am a coward and a non-starter. I want to bring about his restoration to this country and to your arms, and this is very sincere; if the Russians want me in exchange, they can have me.

'As you may know, I was a lieutenant of the Spanish Foreign Legion. If the Russians were to get me in their hands they would certainly shoot me, because they cannot possibly get any military information out of me at my age. Therefore, I will inform the *Daily Express* that I am willing to trade my life for his. Please do not think I have anything to lose. I am a widower and life is lonely.

'You must take it from me, my dear Pat, that the Russians must have given him the sheer hell of a brainwashing. Crabbie was a dedicated Roman Catholic. At one time he even sought ordination for the priesthood – but he was always falling in love with women, particularly one who could overcome his inferiority complex.

'Thank you once again for your letter and, believe me, that I am sincere in offering my liberty in exchange for that of the man whom you love.

'Concerning the Swordstick, I am furious! I myself designed it; and had it made in Toledo especially for him. Upon the presumption of his death, Mr and Mrs Penrose owed me the duty of restoring it to me, the donor, the somewhat costly talisman which I designed and caused to be made especially for him and it should be in your possession. That is my wish and I am willing to take legal action to bring this about. After your own death, My dear Pat, I desire that the Swordstick should be handed to the curator of the Navy Museum or to the Admiralty.

'I must knock off now as I am not sufficiently drunk . . . to continue . . . until tomorrow.

'20 February 1969.

'(Next day) Having read through what I have written – I am very reluctantly forced to the conclusion that I was not at the time altogether sober. To continue, "Crabbie", Bill Nagle and I shared a basement dormitory in the house of friends – just off the Shepherds Bush district for a few joyful months . . . in 1938. Upon command of "Bill" (the eldest among us), "Crabbie" and "Skeff" – I suggested that we now go forth and make night hideous song! Our favourite "boozer" was "The Redan" in Moscow Road (or some place). Later on Bill joined the Palestine police. "Crabbie" returned to sea as the "Pumps and Chips" aboard an oil-tanker – and I delivered a car to an elderly lady in Rapallo, where I stayed for a month . . . then left to fling woo at her daughter in New York – all in vain. Came the war and Bill got himself re-instated in the Indian Army; Crabbie did a Naval course aboard the training ship *President*, moored alongside the Embankment below Westminster and this weary old warrior rejoined the Irish Guards. In the second battle of Monte Cassino, our beloved Bill fell gloriously with the belated rank of "Major", at the head of his Company of Ghurkas. When peace broke out all over the place – "The Admiral" and I got in touch with one another somehow and became some sort of tenants in "The Gate House" – along with an egregious character called Charles Garnet. The rest you almost certainly know better than I do.

'It is most kind of you to request Mr Hutton to send me a copy of – *Commander Crabb is Alive*. The book should evoke a great deal of interest and will certainly "put the cat amongst the pigeons" and cause more than a few cheeks to blush with shame.

'Your kindly wish to see me again is fully reciprocated but it may well have to be postponed for a few months yet – unless the *Express* commissions us to collaborate on a series of articles to be serialised as a sequel to "Commander Crabb etc.". Meanwhile, a very good friend of mine – from whom I withhold no confidences nor secrets – Johnny Culatto . . . who was a Gunner captain on the East Coast during that last piece of international coarseness, may look you up when visiting friends in Bognor. If your publisher or newspaper will only "blow you to the trip" – you might do worse than come out here and seek out those who remember "Crabbie" when he was earning undying glory here on "The Rock". I saw a film wherein Laurence Harvey (a fine actor) tried to give the impression of Lionel Kenneth Crabb. Through no fault of L.H. the film showed nothing about his immediate post-war career as head of Italian frogmen on that island near Venice – nor about the Italian war-widow who volunteered to be "Crabbie's" secretary because he had insisted on her husband's body receiving full naval honours when buried at sea. Crabbie was not only brave but chivalrous!!

    'Yours with kindly remembrances,

    ' "Skeffy".'

Pat said: 'I don't know what they've done with Crabbie, but they should come clean and tell us. He was alive, I know that from all of the help people gave me, but I am not certain he is alive now, you see the last I heard about him was in 1982. Poor old Crabbie.'

The one person who really knew Crabb, both as an 'officer in charge' and as a friend, was Sydney Knowles.

'He was a great man. I'd have followed him anywhere and, during the war, I did, and, as a matter of fact, I even worked for him afterwards.

'As a boss, he would never ask anybody to do anything he would not do himself, in fact if it were dodgy, he'd get dressed in diving gear and go down and do it himself. He seemed to have no fear either in diving or dealing with mines.

'He had a total dislike of rules for rules' sake, and would do things first and answer for them afterwards.

'His people always came top of the list and, when we were in Italy, that included the Italians. He got those divers to work for him, even though we had been trying to eliminate them only a short time before, although, for that matter, they had been having a good go at us. He treated them as he did us, and so got them to do dangerous mine clearing work. I never saw anybody else do that.

'The war was his time, if you see what I mean, it was a big adventure, and he thrived on it. It was probably the happiest time of his life. It is difficult to understand because you would have to have been there to experience it.'

Syd changed the tone of his voice. 'Do you know, I was sickened, really sickened when I read in the press all those things about Crabbie. I think they came from that former wife of his, she did not know or understand him, just cleared off and left him. I knew the man for 13 years and he never, and I mean never, had any strange habits of leaving a diving suit on in bed, or walking about in rubber things. He was a diver and, although he could hardly swim, he was a bloody good one. He was a man's man if you understand.

'The other thing that annoyed me was also about his private life. He was not an alcoholic as many have said. I knew him and was with him up until the last few months, and, yes, he liked a drink. Hell! – we all did, but he was no worse than any of us others. So he liked a drink!

'He also smoked quite heavily, but then that was the accepted thing. At that time, nearly everybody smoked – not like today. But, that made no difference to Crabbie, for as soon as he got underwater, he was a different person. He really was quite at home underwater.

'One thing that can be categorically stated, and that is, Crabbie was not queer [homosexual] – no way. On the other hand, he was not a womaniser, although he had an eye for a beautiful woman.

'I know of the three main women in his life, there was Paola in Italy, Pat you know, and the woman he married. Sorry if that sounds bitter, but she said a lot of bad and untrue things about Crabbie. I read somewhere that she said Crabbie had knocked the boy about, and that made me angry, I even thought about going to see her to sort it out. That was not Crabbie, he had a lot of time for kids, telling them diving stories.

'If you are going to write about Crabbie, then tell the truth, not the sensational rubbish that was and has been bandied about. That isn't the real Crabbie.'

I asked Syd what he thought about the possibility of Crabbie being 'sent in'.

'It's the sort of thing Crabbie would have done in a "flash", that would have been right up his street. You know, he wanted me to go with him on that job, but I had personal problems and couldn't go.

'It wasn't the normal sort of "job", not like we did before, as he was very touchy when he telephoned me, not his usual self, something was up. So yes, he could have done a job like that.

'Thinking about it, one of the Italian divers was Russian, he lived in Italy, but I'm certain he was Russian. You never know, he may have passed information to the Russians, telling them all about the good work he did in Italy. That was fact, he did do a good job.'

'Crabbie was loyal to an extreme!' I said.

'He was,' replied Syd, 'I've seen him in a rage if anyone said anything against the Queen and Country, or King, as it was in the earlier days. That's why it's possible that he would have been "sent in", as it were, for Crabbie was no Communist and I don't think that he'd have joined the Russian Navy like that, without some reason. He could be bloody stubborn you know. He had his "run-ins" with the Communists in Italy, they were called partisans, but they were Communists.'

I told Syd that we had met people who really disliked Crabbie.

'Yes, I can understand that,' he responded. 'Crabbie had a gravelly voice and brisk manner, and for those who did not know him, I can understand that he upset people. Most people liked him and he liked people. He was a "snappy" dresser, and I suppose some people didn't like that.'

'Final thoughts?' I asked.

'I hope that it comes out as to whose body that is at Portsmouth, because it isn't Crabbie. The message from that ship's captain shook me, and I've thought about it over the years, as to who Crabbie may have told and although I have a tiny doubt, I feel that it did come from Crabbie and in that case, yes, he was alive and in Russia. The truth should be made public, because the man was working for the country he loved. He was a hero, was Crabbie.'

One naval officer who knew Crabb during the last years, whilst he was at HMS *Vernon*, and in London, spoke of him in a similar vein.

'He was an inoffensive chap who would do anyone a good turn. He would baby-sit for fellow officers rather than attend official functions, which he loathed. Whilst at HMS *Vernon*, he never had a beard but used to have a bushy piece of hair on the upper cheek bones.

'People spoke of him having red hair, well he didn't, but he used to have his sideburns singed, which was very popular at that period and that gave a red tinge to his hair.

'As far as women were concerned, he was basically shy, certainly not the womaniser that has been portrayed in some quarters, but he did have an eye for a beautiful woman. I recall that women would fuss around him, sort of wanting to look after him and mother him.'

'There were some reports made about him having strange habits,' I mentioned.

'Such as?' responded the officer.

'Well, I understand that his former wife stated that he wore his diving suit in bed and knocked the boy about, and there were other reports said that he was homosexual.'

'What a lot of bloody rot. Be bloody uncomfortable in a hot and foul-smelling diving suit! I've never heard that one. You see, because I was around during the incident, I was moved away rather rapidly, so I did not follow the story, lost touch.

'Crabbie was not queer and he never in the time that I knew him had any strange habits, and the bit about the boy is total rubbish. As you know, the diving branch was a small entity where everybody knew everything about everybody else, so he'd never have kept anything like that quiet. No!, we'd have all known. For another thing, he used to babysit for us fellow officers and if he was "strange" we wouldn't have let him near the house, let alone the kids. No, those statements are absolute rot.

'He was bloody lonely around that period, especially after the marriage split, but they were not suited for each other, so it did not surprise us. She left his belongings stuck in a field while he was away, and just cleared off. He used to go off on odd jobs to who knows where, and I suppose that didn't help. I don't know who he was answerable to.

'At Christmas 1954, I was at HMS *Vernon* and Crabbie was around. He had nowhere to go, so I invited him to spend Christmas Day with my family. He declined, saying that he didn't want to impose on our family day. You see, that's the sort of person he was. I had already invited another officer over for the day so I told him to persuade Crabbie to join us. He did, and Crabbie came. It was a good day, he was great company and enjoyed playing games with the kids, he was a real father figure. He would have liked to have kids of his own.'

'It says in the Navy List of 1956 that Crabbie was still in the Navy during that year and yet he was reported as being a civilian. Do you have any information on that?' I asked.

'Crabbie left the Navy in 1955, Easter I think it was. If he was employed by the secret service, I don't know, but he made it known that he was not happy about going outside [to become a civilian].

'It was a funny business altogether, because nobody really knew what he was up to and he spent a lot of time in London towards the end of his service, so I rarely saw him. He could well have been working for some secret department.

'The two jobs he did in Portsmouth, on the Russian ships, were not "official" naval jobs but organised by some other organisation, that allowed him access to HMS *Vernon*.'

'It is said by many people that the body buried at Portsmouth was not that of Crabb. Do you have any views on that subject?' I asked.

'That's a dangerous one,' the officer replied, 'and I don't want to get involved – I've too much to lose.'

'Do you have any final thoughts?' I enquired.

'Well, he was a bloody decent chap, and I hope that one day the "whole" truth will come out from the Government, and put an end to the nonsense that has been bandied about, but I doubt it.

'I doubt it very much.'

Commander Crabb became Lev Lvovich Korablov, a Soviet naval officer, according to the secret service dossier that found its way to Bernard Hutton. He copied it, then undertook its translation, before returning it to the underground movement.

In its English form, it was submitted as being conclusive evidence that Commander Crabb had been captured by the Russians at Portsmouth, taken to the Soviet Union, brainwashed, and forced to join the Soviet Navy.

Was the dossier a complete fabrication, put together by Hutton or an organisation that sought to exploit Crabb's name, for whatever end? Or was it genuine, a document that was secreted out of the Eastern Bloc into the West, long enough to be copied, before being returned to its place within the files of the Soviet secret service?

This dossier was not the first, nor the last, item of such information to reach Hutton, for his contacts within the Eastern bloc had often supplied secret details, which proved to be correct.

One person sought to find the truth about the dossier and approached Hutton about it. He was told that the dossier was delivered to the newspaper Hutton worked for, *The Empire News*, and arrived on his desk. He read the contents and abided by the terms – that it should be copied, and returned to the originator. He made a complete photocopy of the document. The enquirer asked where this was done and if a receipt was obtained. Hutton said he could not remember where the copying was undertaken and that he did not have a receipt. He was then asked how he returned it to the 'unknown' party. Hutton replied that he could not remember what the arrangements were.

The enquirer said that it was strange that Hutton could not remember any of the most vital details, which placed doubt on the authenticity of the dossier. Hutton claimed that he was guarding a vital source of information which he would not have wished to compromise.

To support Hutton's case, it is a fact that the former head of MI5, Sir Percy Sillitoe, having read the contents of the dossier, confirmed beyond doubt that it was virtually identical to the one held in the files of the British authorities. He was a former long-serving police officer who was appointed head of MI5 during the service's most difficult years of 1946–1953, when Soviet spies were being unearthed at an alarming rate. Openness about his position with MI5 often caused consternation with his superiors and associates in the US secret service. We have found no evidence that his statement was other than genuine and therefore the case that Crabb was captured and possibly 'sent in' is further strengthened.

Bernard Hutton's report states that Crabb was taken from the water and held captive aboard the cruiser. The Russians then waited for any response from the British but none came. Those who reputedly saw the capture, were silenced by the Official Secrets Act.

Crabb was taken to the ship's hospital where he was held prisoner. This is corroborated by interviews with Soviet sailors in Sweden and Egypt. The ship sailed for Russia with Crabb aboard, and, as witnessed by a warship of the Danish Navy, he – or someone – was transferred ashore by helicopter.

The man who saw an object out at sea was trained to see things in the water, for the area where he lived and worked was very sensitive to the military defence forces. His first thoughts were that the object was a seal, as they are often seen around the coast. Unsure of his observation he climbed onto the roof of a building where he was then able to identify the head of a diver. He then saw another, closer this time, but in line. The closest was some 50 metres out to sea with the farthest at some 100 metres; looking down to the beach he saw a third diver crouched amidst the rocks. He was holding a rope, which led out to the other two divers. All were dressed in black rubber suits and the third man ashore was clearly wearing underwater breathing apparatus, which was also black. The observer noted that the wind was blowing, but that it did not affect the movement of the swimmers who remained in a straight line.

When the swimmer on the beach saw that he was being observed, he moved without any sign of hurry, signalling to the others before entering the water. All swam out to sea where, using their underwater breathing equipment, they disappeared below the water's surface. The observer watched the swimmers disappear, then raised the alarm. The ensuing search found no trace of the swimmers, but revealed the marks on the sea bed of a tracked midget submarine, known to be of Soviet design. The tracks led to the keel marks of a larger submarine which was determined to be the mother craft for the smaller vessel.

These swimmers and midget submarines are part of the Soviet Union's élite special forces swimmer brigades which are fully operational throughout the world today, and were in this instance surveying beaches and defensive minefields along Sweden's coastline.

The Soviet Navy had studied in great detail, and with some admiration, the operations carried out by British units of frogmen, charioteers and midget submarines during the war. Britain was, without doubt, a world leader in this field and the operation which found most favour with the Soviets was the midget submarine raid which required the craft to penetrate a well-guarded Norwegian fjord, and its crew to set explosive charges below the German battleship *Tirpitz*. They took a great interest in and had deep respect for the divers who swam ashore prior to amphibious landings, to destroy landing obstructions and remove anti-landing mines. They also had a keen interest in the divers who were involved in countering enemy attacks and removing mines from both the underside of ships and from the bottoms of captured harbours and ports. From those early post-war days, the Russians have foreseen the great advantages of having specially trained underwater operatives, able to undertake underwater operations supported by midget submarines.

Voyska Spetsial Nogo Naznachenniya, or to give it its more common form, *Spetsnaz*, has been a very closely guarded secret since its inception, and full details of its units, both naval and army, have only recently been released after Victor Suvorov, a former Soviet Army officer, defected and provided details. By the end of the 1950s each of the four Soviet fleets is supposed to have had a naval *Spetsnaz* brigade assigned to it, operating directly under the Third Department of the Intelligence Directorate of the GRU.

Because *Spetsnaz* is part of the GRU, the principal military intelligence organisation in the Soviet Union, the ordinary citizen knows virtually nothing about it, nor do most serving military personnel and, indeed, it appears that most *Spetsnaz* units are unaware of the existence of other units, as great precautions are taken to cover up their operations, organisation, strength, function, deployment and even existence. To aid the cover-up all *Spetsnaz* troops wear the same uniforms as the normal Soviet units alongside which they operate. In the case of the naval *Spetsnaz* units, they wear the same uniforms as worn by the Soviet Naval Infantry. Midget submarine crews wear the same uniform as Soviet submariners. In the effort to maintain their anonymity, the *Spetsnaz* brigades do not have separate bases where they could be identified but have guarded compounds within the Naval Infantry bases. *Spetsnaz* troops are denied all contact with civilians or other troops, and all candidates selected for the units undergo checks for loyalty and, upon entry, have to sign a form similar to the Official Secrets Act, the breaching of which is punishable by death.

There are four *Spetsnaz* naval brigades, one assigned to each fleet, and there are four Spetsnaz intelligence units, again one being assigned to each fleet. A brigade consists of up to 1,300 troops and is formed with a headquarters (HQ) company, three combat swimmer/frogmen battalions, a parachute swimmer battalion, a midget submarine group, a signals company and a number of support units.

The combat swimmers and parachutists of the *Spetsnaz* are chosen from the best of those selected for service in the Naval Infantry. They must be trustworthy beyond doubt, for they are required to operate behind enemy lines, in peace as well as in war. Training and continuing service will be demanding and competitive, for promotion is on the basis of the best man for the job, and if one fails to maintain the high standard, there are many others vying to take his place.

The swimmer battalions are for the most part trained in underwater sabotage, mine clearance and intelligence gathering whilst the parachute battalion can perform low altitude drops, combined with amphibious or underwater tasks in the seizure or destruction of maritime targets.

One major aspect of *Spetsnaz* training and operations appears to be centred around dealing with mines, both in disarming them and laying them. Mine phobia is a key factor within Soviet thinking and they place much emphasis on this area of operation. Their interest extends to a careful study of all existing types of mine and they encourage regular handling of them by the units concerned, enhancing their ability to clear paths through minefields to deal with explosive devices fitted to underwater targets and to place mines during underwater attacks.

The *Spetsnaz* naval brigades have to be able to operate in all oceans and in all climates. It is not known whether, once a man joins a particular brigade, he remains with it for his entire service or whether he can be moved to other units. Once trained, the swimmer/ parachutist/midget submariner will be assigned to an operational unit, where training continues and operations begin.

The combined Army and Navy *Spetsnaz* brigades are thought to number some 30,000 troops, both men and women, for covert and specialist operations. During mobilisation in the event of war or crisis, that figure could be increased by calling up reservists, who maintain close links with the organisation after service.

Today, the *Spetsnaz* naval brigades are assigned to covert operations against enemy maritime targets, and to undertake this role they have developed a formidable delivery system of midget submarines, supported by larger parent submarines which have been adapted to carry the small craft to the target area. The combat swimmer frogmen are able to operate from either craft, as both have the ability to 'lock out' and 'lock in' the swimmers whilst remaining submerged.

The training of these élite troops takes place at a number of locations within the Soviet Union, one such centre being at Odessa. The particular relevance of this, which will become apparent, is the fact that it is the centre which specialises in training men to deal with underwater mines, and with demolition. The training requires dedication and it is reported that a high proportion of those selected for the *Spetsnaz* are athletes. There are two specific reasons for this: the first is to make sure the men have the best training and facilities, and the second is to allow them to travel abroad to countries where they may well be expected to operate in war or crisis conditions. The ZSKA sports club sends its athletes all over the world and the fact that they have military rank is not hidden. As the Soviet Union has an extremely large and strong swimmer contingent, it must be assumed that many of the men and women are in turn members of the *Spetsnaz* naval brigades.

In 1945 the Soviets had no combat swimmer units, midget submarines or élite specialist amphibious formations capable of undertaking covert underwater operations. Britain did, and they led the world, having gained a good deal of knowledge from the Italians. After 1945, with no large war requiring 'underwater troops', Britain began to reduce and rationalise the special forces, and as the majority of those operatives were 'hostilities only' they were keen to return to civilian life and take up their former occupations. The story was the reverse in the Soviet Union for they began preparing for future wars, and this included the specialist underwater functions. As already stated, by the end of the 1950s, the Soviets are reputed to have had one *Spetsnaz* brigade assigned to each fleet, and that is no mean feat by any standard. To aid the formation of such establishments, they would have looked outside the Soviet Union and their allies for expertise in such operations, to countries which would be willing to pass on their experience, especially in the combat swimmer role. Apart from the British, the Italians were the forerunners in this type of warfare, with their Tenth Flotilla. After the Allied invasion of Italy, some members joined forces with the Germans whilst others joined the partisans, resulting in some of the Italian swimmers becoming Communists. This could have provided the Soviets with skilled personnel and valuable knowledge of equipment, although it is known that the Allies did block most of their moves.

The Soviet's greatest weakness in 1945 was in underwater mine warfare. This is an area where one has not only to consider the mines, but also the fact that they lie in water, and that very often that water will be murky silt, which means that all handling has to be done by feel. The Russians needed to train their *Spetsnaz* swimmers in the art of attacking maritime targets, by attaching mines to them, and in undertaking reconnaissance missions, during which enemy mines laid for defence purposes may have to be neutralised.

The formation and training of what amounts to literally thousands of combat swimmer frogmen which, apart from those in the *Spetsnaz*, included those supporting naval and amphibious units as well as the Army divers, could not have remained a total secret. British and US intelligence would have become aware that something was happening, but, because the Soviet Union was closed to outsiders, information leaking out would have been very limited. The major concern would have rested with the full knowledge of the threat posed by underwater operatives: intelligence would have been at great pains to find out in some detail the plans and development of such units. The ideal would have been to obtain a defector, but this was obviously unpredictable. The other possibility was that somebody from the West could be infiltrated into the Soviet camp to report on the situation, even if this only provided confirmation of the existence of such units.

The idea of infiltrating somebody into the Soviet Union is not far-fetched, and it would have been a top priority.

There have been a number of infiltration operations against the Soviet Union. One such incident described in the *Dictionary of Espionage* by Christopher Dobson and Ronald Payne is that of Zigurd Krummins. He was an anti-Russian Latvian who had escaped the Soviet occupation and returned in 1952 after being spirited into Estonia from a British trawler. He joined up with an underground movement and undertook espionage and sabotage missions against the Russians. He operated for almost two years before being caught by the Soviet security service, whereupon he was charged as a traitor and spy, to be sentenced to fifteen years' imprisonment. As with Crabb, completion of sentence did not mean a return to the West. A recent book by Tom Bower, *The Red Web* (Aurum Press, 1989), also describes how MI6 sent in a string of agents to operate in the Baltic states; catastrophically the whole network was penetrated by the KGB.

During the mid-1950s intelligence departments in Britain and the USA would certainly have explored the feasibility of an infiltration operation, daring in concept, but vital if the Soviets were in the process of forming élite frogmen units. On the other side, the Soviets would not miss the opportunity to recruit a frogman with skills and knowledge that they could utilise, if one were available. NATO intelligence would have considered it probable that the right person would have some chance of survival at least long enough to gain some knowledge of Soviet intentions. Intelligence planners would have realised that the person would need to win some Soviet confidence and arrive in a position where he could get any useful information. They would also have considered the fact that, once the Russians had made good use of that person or found out what was going on, there would be little time to get him out, and at worst he would have to be left to his own fate. With any luck the intelligence department would gain enough information to make a good assessment, while for the operative the risk would simply be part of being in the service of his country.

Selecting a suitable candidate for such an operation would not be straightforward. He would need to hold a fairly senior rank and have a well-known past, for the Soviets set great store by operational experience when assessing the importance of their military staff, and that would be no exception in this case. The operative's record of underwater operations would need to be impeccable and a strong familiarity with mines and demolitions a priority, for he would have to pass on some information to the Russians; that, however, would be of little consequence compared with the information he stood to gain. The candidate would need to be single with no strong family ties, and he would need to be loyal beyond any shadow of doubt. He would also have to be fully aware of the risks involved, for it would be a most daring and dangerous operation.

Most frogmen, charioteers and midget submarine crews of the Second World War period had been demobilised; they were in civilian occupations and had families. They were part of society again, and, even if their knowledge and experience were valuable, they would be missed if they disappeared. But one man did fit the requirements. He had a glowing record of service during and after the war, he was an underwater mine warfare expert and he had worked for naval intelligence. Divorced, and with no close family ties except for his mother, he was loyal to an extreme and would undertake the job without hesitation. From his dealings with the intelligence service he had the basis of a cover, and this could be expanded upon. He was extremely valuable to the British and he would be a viable prize for the Soviets.

Commander Lionel Kenneth Philip Crabb, RNVR, GM, OBE, was available for such an operation and would have accepted such a challenge without a second thought.

The Russians would have explored all possibilities in trying to gain the expertise required and, when the opportunity arose to capture one of the world's best, they prepared and activated a plan to seize him. Once they had trapped him, they could keep him, at least long enough to avail themselves of vital data.

They knew, from their informants in the British security services, that they were dealing with a very stubborn man, who had blind loyalty to his country, and so the plan would have to be of such a nature that it appeared to Crabb that he was being sent in by his own people to undertake a spying mission. Once he found out the truth, it would be too late and they would deal with him, depending upon his response, at the time.

The first task that would befall Crabb – Korablov, once he had accepted his position and joined the Soviet Navy, would have been to learn Russian. The language course designed for such an event would have been thorough and very demanding. He would have settled down to the job as it was part of his 'cover' requirement and necessary to pure survival. Once he had learnt enough Russian to be of use, he would have begun what he would have thought of as the beginning of his secret mission. He was, according to the records, sent to a Soviet Naval Training Centre where he began his career as Lev Lvovich Korablov.

During the first part of his induction into the ways of the Soviet Navy, he would have maintained a very low profile, with security observation continuous. To those around him, he would have been the naval officer with the strange accent and pronunciation. Some might also have thought it odd for a man of his age to be undergoing training courses.

Once the initial phase was complete, he would have had his diving skills and knowledge tested. During this time he could well have been given numerous items of equipment to test and report on. It could be assumed that any reports given would have been critical and scathing to the extreme, but the Russians would have listened and analysed. They would also have been testing him to assess his attitude to his new role.

Crabb was a hero, his wartime service and decorations showed that. The Russians have made a policy of introducing veterans of World War Two to new intakes of Soviet servicemen: the veterans give lectures about their struggles defending the motherland against great odds and with huge losses, hoping to implant in the young recruits the idea that it is now their turn to defend their land against the aggressor. In Crabb's case, he would have lectured about the defence of Gibraltar, about Italy and new advances in underwater warfare. The students would have been keen to listen. It would not have mattered that the students before him were aware that he had a strange accent and had served with the British during the war, for these were the trusted ones, the Soviet Union's new élite.

The underground organisation in Eastern Europe and the Soviet Union which had provided Hutton with the secret dossier now began to provide precise details, albeit by irregular methods, of Crabb – Korablov's career. According to Hutton's informants, Crabb – Korablov visited each of the Soviet Navy's main fleet bases, all of which were in the process of establishing *Spetsnaz* swimmer units. It is of great interest to note that all reports coming out of Russia told of his involvement with special task divers/frogmen: this information was made known long before the West had any knowledge of the *Spetsnaz*.

The posting that has been recorded, which is of particular interest, is that when he was sent to the Soviet Naval Command at Odessa, for it is at this base that the Soviets developed their underwater mine and explosives warfare training centre. It is therefore a main centre for the *Spetsnaz* combat swimmer training, in demolition and mine warfare.

This may well have been Crabb – Korablov's first contact with the *Spetsnaz* operational staff and he would be aware that these divers and swimmers were different from those he had met previously. They would have worn normal naval uniform, with nothing to denote that they were part of an élite force.

As far as Crabb was concerned it would have been a revival of the Italian days. It was the thing that had inspired him most, the challenge and the adventure. Here there was no war, but he was part of a great military machine, designing, developing, training and equipping divers and swimmers. He would have been in his element and, of course, gathering a vast amount of vital information.

He would also have wondered if he would ever see his friends in the West again.

Hutton's contact then reported that Crabb – Korablov had been sent to Sevastopol which was the base for the Black Sea Naval Command, and was out of reach of European underground organisations – should the West have decided to get Crabb out. At Sevastopol Crabb – Korablov took command of the Special Underwater Operation Group, which was certainly *Spetsnaz*. His movements in this area were also verified through the entirely independent source of Pat Rose's 'woman of Turkey'.

Crabb – Korablov would have been aware at an early stage that things were not as they should be. The KGB had told him that a body had been found, identified as his, and then buried. He knew that the authorities wanted the story of his disappearance to melt away. He was faced with a long term in the Soviet Navy – for it was soon apparent that he was not going to be extricated, but left to his own devices. Obviously the Russians would not have told him anything about their infiltration of the British security services, nor that they set up his capture. A mystery almost as large as the Crabb affair itself was the flow of anonymous messages into the West over the years. Who really sent them? The photographs were not conclusive, neither were the reports. The written letter which Pat Rose requested never appeared. However, much of what was said in telephone calls was verified from other unconnected sources, and the message Syd Knowles received from Captain Myelkov was dramatically convincing.

How was this information gathered, who had contact with Crabb, who had his trust and was able to keep contact throughout the vast expanse of the Soviet Union? People here said that it was the 'Soviet information service'. This could be accepted just after the event, for it caused great embarrassment to the British Government, but for the reports to continue over the years with a growing number of verifiable facts seems to provide strong evidence that Crabb and Korablov were indeed the same person.

10

The Problems

Bernard Hutton was a Czechoslovakian emigré who had established himself as a reporter within a London newspaper group. He was credited with having good underground contacts in Russia and Eastern Europe. It is through these secret organisations that he obtained the evidence that Crabb and Korablov were one and the same person.

I have been asked on more than one occasion whether I believe in the secret reports that were supposed to have been smuggled out of the Soviet Union and forwarded to him. I have to answer that I don't know. In his books, Hutton recounts conversations that quite frankly he could not have any record of. On the other hand much of what he wrote has a ring of truth about it.

I, in turn, asked others for their views of the author's work. I met with replies which ranged from 'pure fabrication' to: 'He would ask a question, and if the answer was not what he wanted he would ask the question a different way, until he had the answer he wanted. He was clever like that.' What cannot be argued with is the fact that Hutton wrote a number of books depicting Crabb in Russia, but there have been none countering these allegations.

Until his death Bernard Hutton continued to receive information from his contacts in the Eastern bloc. Then came the dramatic news that Crabb was going to retire from the Soviet Navy and be released into Italy. The report stated that Italy was his own choice. That dramatic news also reached Pat Rose through her 'woman of Turkey' contact. The unidentified voice merely stated that Commander Crabb was to leave Russia and go to live in Italy.

The events surrounding Crabb's release to the West are described in detail in the next chapter, but it is interesting at this point to review the events that surrounded both Hutton and Rose during those days of tension and illness.

Amid the continuing supply of information and latest good news reaching Hutton, he also suffered setbacks, none more so than when he received unwelcome visitors. He wrote to Pat Rose about them in 1974. 'To top it all, in October I had a break-in into my study; they broke the glass in the French door and got in. Apart from very valuable cameras, tape recorders, recordings, films, pictures, etc., they also took EVERY piece of paper; they skilfully unlocked my "safety locked" steel desk, emptied the drawers, took scripts, address and note books with phone numbers, and even emptied all my files containing correspondence. So I am left without any records and for some odd reason I just couldn't remember your exact address.

'I know, and am convinced, it's all the work of the KGB or their agents because of the recent publicity about Crabbie coming back; they probably wanted to find out who my contacts behind the Iron Curtain are, but this they didn't find because it's not kept at the bungalow.'

It was a tragic blow for both of them, for Pat Rose had loaned Hutton letters, notes and photographs, and now they were gone. We asked Pat if she had ever had a break-in, and she told us that she didn't have anything of value to either the KGB or MI5 for that matter, as everything of interest had been with Hutton. Before he died, however, he did send material back to her which had not been kept at the bungalow and that proved to be of great value to our research.

Before this, however, news had continued to flow to Hutton, confirming that Crabb was to be released, and this was corroborated by an independent source who wrote to Pat Rose with this information: 'It was the Italians who told me there were rumours – from very reliable sources – that Crabbie will have his Russian contract ended in the spring of 1976 and that there is every possibility it might be in 1975 because of his "good record". They added that the same sources said he planned to come to Italy and not to England and made attempts to find out whether or not he would be allowed to stay there. As soon as I had this information, I immediately contacted my reliable people to find out what the position is and to let me have every detail about Captain Korablov (Crabbie) they can. I had now a "signal" that a "full report is on its way" and, as I fear that it could be intercepted if it came by mail, I made arrangements to have it handed over to me; I expect this to be either this Thursday when I am in London or latest the following week. I have no clue what this report contains, but I do know that it comes from my sources who always provide me with impeccable information. We'll soon know.'

Apart from the break-in, Hutton believed that his phone was being tapped and his mail intercepted. It is possible that he was under surveillance by both sides, for his revelations could be doubly embarrassing. Again he wrote to Pat about his concerns and they developed a code that they could use as their investigations developed into what they hoped would be the culmination of years of work and research. Hutton wrote to Pat Rose: 'I didn't want to tell you all this over the phone because I know that my phone is tapped since the Italian TV matter arose when they told us Crabbie was to be released, and I don't want to give anything away. I'll be back home from London very late on Thursday, so don't phone me that night, but if you can ring Friday night – the best would be around 7 pm. If I have it, the code to let you know will be "Harry sends you his regards"; if the report contains anything really good – I mean very concrete up-to-date information about Crabbie – I'll tell you "Harry sends you his regards and will be ringing to arrange when you could have lunch with him." '

The information did arrive and the later message reached Pat, when a meeting was arranged. Hutton passed Pat the details. But as good news arrived, so did bad in the form of ill health for Hutton, and it began to play a part in the drama. He wrote of it to Pat: 'I am somewhat worried about my health because the consultant told me that if the present treatment doesn't produce rapid results the only way to get me back to normal would be another operation. Anyway, as you see, this bloody painful illness does not get me down and will NOT prevent me from working.'

Hutton waited for news to arrive from the Eastern bloc, and at the same time fought against poor health. He maintained contact with

Pat, by letter rather than using the telephone. His letters showed a determined desperation to gather the final details: 'The only later news I got was: that he had, in fact, left Russia, had fallen ill in East Germany (Dresden) on his journey to Italy and was sent to Czechoslovakia (Karlovy Vary) for treatment. That was the last news I had, but I am doing everything I can to try to get further (and preferably up-to-date) news. Here again, as soon as I get anything I shall be in touch with you.'

Mrs Rose had not restricted her search for Crabbie to the official bodies, she contacted anybody who she thought could help. One such person was Mr J. Hunter who lived in Eastbourne and was a medium of some international repute; Pat sent him an article which had been written outlining the events of the Crabb saga. His reply is quoted in full and dated 14 February 1978:

'Dear Mrs Rose,

'Many thanks for your letter and enclosure. I have read the article in the magazine but I preferred to answer your questions first in case I was influenced by it.

'The grave definitely does not contain the body of Commander Crabb. I delved into the identity of the person there and, as I see it, the body, which was chosen for its physical similarities, was taken from a mortuary very shortly after death and, having been prepared, was discovered. After a post mortem and inquest it was placed in the grave.

'As to the woman who placed the flowers on the grave for so long, there is no close association with the one buried there. As near as I can get it her part in the whole affair was undertaken from a point of duty.*

'As to who arranged the whole matter. That question I prefer not to answer since there is a strong feeling of viciousness there, and the further one keeps from aspects such as that the more peaceful life is going to be.

'I can assure you that if you try to bring this matter into the open once again you will have cause to rue it. One cannot fight atom bombs with a bow and arrow.

*This point becomes relevant later in the book, as neither the writer nor Pat Rose knew who the woman was.

'The time will come when the whole matter will come out into the open, but that is several years away yet.

'Commander Crabb's feelings concerning this matter have very much changed over the years. In the beginning he felt very bitter when he realised that his life's future had been taken out of his hands.

'However, he realises nothing can be done about it and so he has resigned himself to the fact that it has happened to others too; he was just another one on the list.

'His feelings are that had the whole affair taken place at the present time then the whole outcome would have been entirely different.

'He does think very tenderly often of what might have been, and finds his present life very much lacking in the things he had planned.

'He is not unhappy, but then he is not happy either. His ambitions have gone by the board, and he is fully aware that, if someone waved a magic wand and enabled him to come back to this country, he would have nothing here to look forward to. So he has resigned himself and is doing his best to make something of his life with what is to hand.

'I have since read the article and can see no reason to alter anything that I have sensed.

> 'Yours sincerely
> J. Hunter (Mr)'

Mr Hunter has since moved to Australia, and Pat had no further contact with him. But she certainly had been fighting atom bombs with a bow and arrow, and had fought to seek the truth even though she may well have rued the day.

Pat was even more convinced that Commander Crabb was alive and in Russia. Reports still came, saying that he was well and looked forward to their reunion. She could never be absolutely certain that the messages were from Crabbie, even when they contained details that were not common knowledge. She maintained her determination to find the truth, inspired by the evidence of Sydney Knowles, the meeting with Ken Elliott, the information from Bernard Hutton, and the 'lady of Turkey'.

She decided to take the matter to Parliament again and wrote to

Martin Flannery, the Member of Parliament for Sheffield (Hillsborough), as he had a reputation for dealing with such cases.

Her letter, dated 20 November 1979, reads:

'Dear Mr Flannery,

'With the names of all the bonnie ex-varsity defectors from this country to Russia being brought into circulation once more, may I suggest to you another name you might like to bring forward in the House – no defector he, nor ex-varsity nor homo; just a simple and extremely brave sailor – Commander Crabb. He did not give away his country's secrets nor sell them: he did a dangerous underwater job for his faceless masters at Portsmouth on 19 April 1956, was betrayed by a double agent and captured and taken to Russia a prisoner.

'It has been said but without true foundation (for the body buried in his name was not his) that he died there but I have abundant evidence to the contrary that he survived and was employed in the Russian Navy (photographic evidence of this).

'He was a victim of the all-high super-establishment of security bosses; he was sent on this errand and, having been captured, was ignored and no-one wants to know about him any more – typical drill.

'How about getting some particulars of his present whereabouts? How about getting him back to this country, his England to which he was always a brave, loyal and devoted subject?

'The late Colonel Marcus Lipton (Lab. Brixton) tried to raise his question in the House but was refused; perhaps you will be more fortunate now, if you care to bring his story up.

'Why do I want to know? Because at the time of his disappearance I was engaged to be married to him.

'Yours sincerely . . .'

She received a promising reply to her letter, dated 26 November 1979:

'Dear Mrs Rose,

'Than you for your letter of 20 November 1979 about Commander Crabb.

'You have my deepest sympathy concerning the events of many

years ago, but surely, if you have evidence that the Commander is still alive – and you are categoric in this statement – you really ought to furnish some of us with it.

'If you were to give me such evidence I would certainly use it in order to arrive at the truth, which always seems to be a casualty in these cases.

'Kindest regards,

'Yours sincerely,
'Martin Flannery, MP.
'*Hillsboro*' *Sheffield*'

Having established contact, she set out the basis for the evidence, which she considered should have generated some interest. Her letter was dated 8 December 1979:

'Dear Mr Flannery,
'Many thanks for your courteous letter of 26 November.
'Concerning the evidence of Commander Crabb being alive, I would ask you to read some parts of the books I enclose.
'1. *The Fake Defector* pp. 139 – 148: the man referred to as V.N. was actually a Mr Kenneth Elliott whom I met in London: he had been working for some 20 years for Lucas; he gave me the telephone number of his office in Grosvenor Street: it seems he went to Russia for his firm to sell buses, but when I tried to contact him by telephone, I was told that he had left the firm and gone no-one knew whither – this after 20 years with the firm!
'2. *International History* Magazine pp. 26 – 32: With regard to the body buried under Commander Crabb's name, his lifelong friend and diving companion, Sydney James Knowles, said the body was not Crabb's but he was over-persuaded later by authority under the Official Secrets Act to deny this and agree that it was his body. Some four years after this, he got in touch with me and said that he knew how very fond of me the Commander was and that he felt he could no longer stay silent and must tell me that his evidence identifying the body was untrue.
'I apologise for inflicting so much literature on you but I do

hope that if you can spare the time to go through these pages, you may come to the same conclusion as I that Crabb is alive in Russia.

'Will you please, at your convenience, let me have the two books back.

'Yours sincerely,
'Mrs Pat Rose.

'PS Mr J. Bernard Hutton, the author of *The Fake Defector*, has the recorded tape of Knowles' evidence.'

She received confirmation that her detailed letter had reached the right person:

'19 December 1979
'Dear Mrs Rose,
'Mr Flannery has asked me to thank you for the books you have sent him which he will return when he has had the opportunity to read them.

'This may take some time but he says he feels you will understand.

'Yours sincerely,
'*Secretary to MP.*'

Pat Rose heard nothing again until she received a letter dated 30 April 1980 from the MP's office, stating that he still had the matter in hand:

'Dear Mrs Rose,
'I am afraid that circumstances have prevented me doing anything regarding the case of Commander Crabb, but I have not forgotten the matter.

'Please give me a month or two as I just have not had time to read the material you sent me in what has been a quite hectic exhausting political year.

'Kindest regards,
'pp Martin Flannery, MP
'*Hillsboro' Sheffield.*'

It was six months later when the next letter of any significance arrived, and this merely stated that the enquiry was being forwarded to the Home Office for their report:

'27 October 1980
'Dear Mrs Rose,
'Thank you for your letter of 20 October 1980. I am sorry to say that your reminder was very necessary and I feel quite guilty that I have let the matter slip.
'I have now however, as a result of your latest letter, sent photostats of your letters of 8 December and 20 November 1979 to the Home Secretary to ask for his comments. This is always a good prelude to raising a matter publicly and I will let you have a copy of his comments when I receive them.
'As the Home Office is notoriously the slowest department of state to react, due to the many individual cases it handles, this will take some time.
'Could I finally ask you one question which springs from Parliamentary protocol and convention, have you raised the matter with your own MP?
'Kindest regards,

'Yours sincerely,
'Martin Flannery, MP
'*Hillsboro' Sheffield.*'

The next letter that Pat Rose received was dated 19 November 1980. This was a letter that Martin Flannery had received from the Home Office, just over a month after his enquiry, and their response was to pass on the subject to the Ministry of Defence:

'HOME OFFICE
'QUEEN ANNE'S GATE LONDON SW1H 9AT

'10 NOV 1980

'Thank you for your letter to the Home Secretary of 30 October enclosing one from Mrs Pat Rose about the disappearance of Commander Crabb in April 1956.

'After interdepartmental consultations, it appears that this is more a matter for the Ministry of Defence, so I have sent your letter there with a request that a reply be sent to you direct. I apologise for the delay.

> 'MRS K.I. ELAM
> '*Private Office.*'

With all of the evidence that had been placed before the various governmental departments, the Ministry of Defence had the final say. The letter was forwarded via Martin Flannery, who did not write himself but only placed a compliment slip in with it. The words of interest are, 'considered missing and presumed dead'. Surely if Pat Rose could submit evidence that might have thrown light on the Crabb affair, it should be looked at, and not swept aside by a short letter, unless of course there was more to the story than is admitted. The contents of the letter were the final official words.

'MINISTRY OF DEFENCE
'MAIN BUILDING WHITEHALL
'LONDON SW1A 2HB

'The Parliamentary Under-Secretary of State for Defence for the Royal Navy

'N/US.379/80   28 November 1980

'Dear Mr Flannery,
    'Your letter dated 30 October addressed to the Home Secretary has been referred to me.
    'As you will know, Commander Crabb was considered missing, presumed dead when he failed to return from a diving exercise at Portsmouth on the morning of 19 April 1956. Fourteen months later a headless corpse, dressed in a diving suit similar to that worn by Crabb, was washed ashore at Chichester harbour, and at the inquest the coroner stated that he was satisfied that the remains were those of Crabb. The family solicitors also took the view that Crabb was dead.
    'Mrs Pat Rose's conviction that Crabb is alive and living in Russia was published in the *Sunday Mirror* on 15 September 1974. The

Ministry of Defence had no evidence then, nor does it now, to suggest that a mistake had been made about Crabb's death. I do not therefore consider that any further enquiry into the matter would be justified.

'Yours sincerely,
'Keith Speed.'

Pat Rose was not prepared to accept this final response, and wrote again, laying out details, which surely the authorities could have answered. It was dated 11 December 1980 and read as follows:

'Dear Mr Flannery,

'Thank you for copy of Defence Ministry letter of 28 November wherein the death of Crabb is accepted as being established: I have reason to disbelieve this.

'Firstly, at the time the headless body turned up at Chichester, there were certain experts on the local tides who declared that a body lost in April 1956 would have been swept far out to sea by June 1957.

'Secondly, a companion diver and close friend of Crabb, Sydney James Knowles BEM, has declared on a recording tape how, when asked to identify this body, he was unable to do so and, when recalled, was still certain it was not Crabb (few men would have more detailed knowledge of each other's bodies than diving mates who were frequently together in a state of nakedness): finally he was over-persuaded under some pressure to agree to the identification of this body as being Crabb's and was told that this came under the Official Secrets Act. A few years later Knowles decided the truth must be told of his part in this affair, which was now preying on his mind and even affecting his health, so he made the recording referred to.

'Thirdly, a Mr Kenneth Elliott, who held a position for many years with the firm of Lucas, told me in London in 1968 that he had just returned from a trip to Russia for Messrs Lucas and that, when in Sevastopol, he had observed some frogmen emerging from the sea and his guide/interpreter said, "Look, there is your famous Commander Crabb".

'Perhaps the above information, such as it is, may encourage you

[137]

to pursue your enquiries into Crabb's present whereabouts (at least I hope so) and, if he is in Russia, to try and obtain his release.

'Yours sincerely,
'Mrs Pat Rose
'PS Happy Christmas!'

To this day, Pat never received any acknowledgement to this letter, which confirms to her the fact that the Crabb case was not all it was purported to be to the general public.

11

The Solution

During 1974 messages arrived from Italy, indicating that Crabb could possibly be released into Italy in 1976. Both Bernard Hutton and Pat Rose received the same message, from different sources, and both investigated the possibilities that it might happen.

Hutton told Pat that he had heard, and confirmed through his contacts, that Crabb's contract was to terminate in August 1976 and that he would retire from Russian military service. He also said that there was a possibility that he could complete his service a year earlier, retaining all of his retirement rights.

Pat Rose received a telephone call from a man, who identified himself by using the phrase the 'woman in Turkey'. He told her that he and his associates had heard that Crabb was to retire from the Soviet Navy, and would be allowed to go to Italy. He told her to be ready to depart for Italy as soon as they had more news, so that she could once again join him.

Hutton's contacts sent more details of Crabb's release and he told Pat that Crabbie was asked where he would like to retire and live after completion of his service. He was asked whether it would be in the USSR or in a Western country. Crabb had, of course, been in the Soviet Union for 18 years by this time and had adapted to their way of life. He did, however, retain his strong affection for Italy, and Hutton told Pat that Crabb said he would like to spend the remainder of his days there.

Pat thought that the message was logical and agreed that it could well be Crabbie's wish, for she appreciated that he might well feel very bitter about the country that he had once loved and served. (She had also been told by her own contacts that Crabb would go to Italy.)

Hutton's next communication to Pat about the release came when he heard that the Russians had made a discreet approach to Rome, to seek out the Italian authorities' views as to whether they would allow Crabb to live in their country. Rumours of this had begun to spread, but Hutton explained to Pat that the authorities in Rome had neither confirmed nor denied the rumours.

The world's media soon displayed great interest in the possibility of Crabb's being released and they contacted both Pat and Hutton to gain first-hand insight into the story. Pat Rose told us that RAI, an Italian television company which had made a very successful film about Crabb in the 1960s, sent a production team to Britain to interview Hutton and herself. As part of the programme, the producer approached the Admiralty for their views on the latest developments in the Crabb affair. They still maintained their original stance: 'We are making no comment.'

Mrs Rose said that the Russians were taken by complete surprise over the way their 'softly softly' approach to Rome had leaked and generated so much international interest. They were also embarrassed, for they had not finally agreed to allow Crabbie to leave Russia and live in the West. She was told that the Russians then decided to confuse the Western media and made enquiries, quite openly, to the governments of Turkey, Sweden, France and West Germany, as to whether they would accept Crabbie if he were to be released. News of the enquiries reached the media and Pat heard that there was total confusion as to where Crabbie was going to turn up.

'I knew that it was to be Italy, for I had been told by my contact through Turkey and they had been right on a number of things in the past, and of course, Bernard Hutton had also been told through a totally separate source,' she declared.

Pat waited for more news; when it came it was from Hutton. He confirmed that his sources now stated that Crabb had agreed with the Russians to complete his contract, which meant one more year in naval service, and as was his wish, he would retire from military service on 17 August 1976. It had also been decided and confirmed, explained Hutton, that Crabb would be permitted to leave the Soviet

Union in 1977 and be free to live in Italy as he had requested.

The Russians for their part are supposed to have made the demand that upon his release from the Soviet Union he must never return to Britain or go to the United States of America, and to comply with that demand he would have to sign a state paper, agreeing to these conditions.

Pat Rose was thrilled at the news. She explained, 'Crabbie would agree to the restricted travel demand for he would not want to return to his England, the country that he probably felt had dumped him for a vital mission. No, Italy was a country that he loved, and that is where he would want to go.' At last she would be able to join him.

Hutton further explained to Pat that his report stated that Crabbie would be required to live for six months at a place where he would be conditioned for his return to the West, for he had spent a long time in Russia and would be unfamiliar with the modern Western world. He would receive his full pension of $10,000 per annum, to be paid weekly, as this should allow him to live comfortably in retirement. He would in addition receive a grant prior to his departure to enable him to purchase clothes and personal items, so that he was appropriately dressed and equipped for his new life in the West.

Pat asked Hutton if he thought that Crabbie really would be released to the West, because he knew so much about the Russian divers and their bases. Hutton explained that Crabb would always remain under the control of the Russians, who would keep a careful watch on him. One thing he could not explain, though, was the legal implications of a captured British citizen, taken to the Soviet Union, kept for 21 years, forced to serve in the Soviet Navy and then retired to a Western Alliance country. What for instance was to be his nationality – British, Russian or Italian? Would not the British and American intelligence organisations immediately recapture him for debriefing?

Hutton reiterated the fact that everybody who leaves the Soviet Union is under no misapprehension about the length of the arm of the KGB, who would go to extreme lengths to eliminate anybody who stepped out of line. The Russians were placing a lot of faith in the view that Crabb would not run to the British authorities and it is probable that the Soviets would already have convinced Crabb that the British had dumped him. Hutton finished by saying everything was now ready for Crabbie's release.

It was in February 1976 that Pat Rose contacted Bernard Hutton with her own latest information. 'I have really good news that has come from Crabbie, Joe! (Hutton was known to his friends as Joe.) The message is genuine, I know it is, I have no doubt about it. I know now, from him, that I shall see him again. It seems that it hasn't been decided when he will be allowed to leave Russia, but it will be some time next year.'

Again it was a matter of waiting, and it was agonising for Pat Rose since although she had received messages she could not know if they were completely reliable: all she could do was wait for the word that he was actually in Italy, and hope that the caller was not playing a cruel hoax. Pat next heard from Hutton, who told her that it was confirmed through a report he had received that Crabb would leave the Soviet Union in 1977. His informants stated that it was believed that Commander Crabb/Korablov would travel to the West, probably to Italy, in either June or August 1977, but Commander Crabb would definitely reappear in the West.

In July 1977 Hutton contacted Pat and told her he had just received a message through his contacts in the Soviet Union: Crabbie would be leaving the Soviet Union on 3 or 4 August to travel to Italy. Shortly after being contacted by Hutton, Pat received a telephone call. A voice told her that he was speaking for the 'woman in Turkey', and that Commander Crabb was to arrive in Italy on 3 or 4 August. The phone then went dead as was the normal practice so she had no time to ask his identity or any other details. She still lived in the belief that these calls were genuine, and telephoned Hutton to tell him about this latest one. The details were now confirmed by two independent sources.

It was on Tuesday 26 July 1977 that Hutton contacted Mrs Rose. He was very excited, for he said that he had just received very good news from his informants that, on 3 or 4 August, Captain Korablov/Commander Crabb would arrive in East Germany (DDR) with two members of the Soviet security service. The exact date was to depend upon suitable transport. He would then travel with the two security officers to Italy, where he would remain under their supervision, under the guidance of Moscow.

Pat asked if he had any idea when she would be able to travel to Italy and see him. Hutton could not answer her question for he had no idea of the route to Italy or where Crabb would live. He also told her that the Soviet security would be very stringent because of the deep interest shown by the Western media. 'Do you think he will be allowed to give a press conference?' Pat pressed, but Hutton could only say that he had no information about any media involvement. Whatever was decided would certainly be to the Russians' advantage, he was sure. It was certain that for the initial period at least Crabb would be kept under very close scrutiny and would not be allowed to go anywhere without an escort. He said that it might well be possible for her to see him, but left it that he would call her as soon as he had any further details.

The next communication that Pat received came from a friend of hers who was a high-ranking intelligence officer, whose identity cannot be revealed. He explained to her that Crabbie was no longer in the Soviet Union and was in fact on his way to Italy. He then told her that he had no further information he could give her, but stressed that what he had told her was official. For Pat, it was another link in the chain confirming that Crabbie was alive and on his way out of Russia.

Pat told us that she became worried when five weeks had passed and neither she nor Hutton had received any further information. Hutton expressed his concern that the KGB may have discovered his informants and that a link in the chain was broken. If that was the case there was nothing he could do but wait.

It was to be ten weeks before Pat was told by Hutton that the message he was waiting for had arrived. Captain Korablov/ Commander Crabb had arrived in Dresden at approximately 01.00 hours on 4 August. With his two Soviet security officers, he was driven to a house on the outskirts of Dresden which was observed to be used by the East German security service (which is in fact the counterpart of, and in part controlled by, the KGB). It was also reported that, during his stay at the house, he did not leave the premises for the first five days. On the sixth day he was escorted on a three-hour walk in the countryside. The following day, at about 08.30, a black car was observed to stop at the house where it collected Crabb and his security officers. It took them at speed to the Soviet HQ in Dresden where, it was said, travel and identity documents were issued to Crabb. Hutton explained that the documents were false, although produced at an official level. It is thought that this action was taken as a way of helping to counter any security leakages.

Naturally Pat was pleased to hear that things were happening, but she was disturbed by the other news that Hutton passed on to her. He told her that the report stated that Crabb/Korablov had reported sick, complaining of severe colic in his stomach and abdomen. It was reported that he felt giddy and his legs gave way when he tried to stand up. He also had a high fever and complained that his body ached all over. His security officers were concerned and a doctor was called to the house. He examined Crabb and then prescribed some drugs, ordering that he should stay in bed for a few days.

Pat was deeply concerned at the news and asked Hutton if he thought that it was a ploy so that the Russians could say he was too unwell to return to the West. Hutton didn't know for he could only rely on his contacts, people who had to undertake the dangerous job of watching over an efficient and ruthless security service. They then had to channel that information through a network of communications links for it to reach the West.

Crabb's health did not improve and the doctor, who made more visits, recommended that he be taken to hospital for examination by a specialist. The security officers would have had to make contact with their superiors in Moscow but it was agreed that he should be admitted to hospital and an ambulance was sent to collect him. At the hospital he underwent checks and X-rays before a thorough specialist examination. The results of these examinations showed that he had ulcers and some cancerous growths in the abdomen, as well as a very low blood circulation.

This was dramatic and worrying news for both Pat and Hutton, for both had previously been told that he was in good health, and nothing had been reported when he had his regular medical checks in the Russian naval hospitals. The report ended by saying that more information would be provided as soon as was practicable.

Crabb/Korablov underwent treatment in the hospital and subsequent reports stated that his condition improved, but there were differences in opinion over whether he should be operated upon or whether the current prescribed treatment should be continued. After consultation within the hospital and with Moscow it was decided that Crabb should not be operated upon because of possible complications. However, it was decided that he should at the earliest opportunity be transferred to a hospital at Karlovy Vary in nearby Czechoslovakia, which specialised in his medical condition.

Pat had no corroborative evidence passed to her during this period, so she relied upon Hutton's reports, which came in written form, in Russian, and therefore needed to be translated. (Apparently Hutton spoke and wrote Russian and was therefore able to undertake his own translation.) She saw both the original and the translated versions, but had to accept the translation at face value, since she had no way of checking its accuracy.

At his next meeting with Pat Rose, Hutton reported that Crabb had remained in the Dresden Hospital for six weeks, and then was given specialist approval for his move from Dresden to Karlovy Vary. It appeared from the report that Crabb was very ill and the delay was made so that he could build up his strength before undertaking the journey.

Crabb departed Dresden Hospital, accompanied by two security officers on the morning of 30 September 1977 to travel to the special state medical centre Karlovy Vary. They arrived in the early evening, having made a slow, careful journey, with a number of 'rest' stops.

Now deeply concerned at the news, Pat saw her hopes of seeing Crabbie again diminishing fast. She asked Hutton what he thought, and he felt that news was not good, but he added that, as the reports stated they were treating him, they had to be hopeful. Pat was not comforted and wondered whether the Russians had known about the medical problems all along, while building up Crabb's hopes of going to Italy. She thought that the Soviet secret service was cruel enough to do that, especially if they didn't want him talking to the media once he had left Russia.

The experienced cancer specialists at Karlovy Vary agreed with the diagnosis found by their German colleagues at Dresden, after having studied the X-rays and medical reports and concluded their own examinations. They prescribed a course of treatment which, if effective, should enable Crabb to live a fairly trouble-free life, but he would have to stick to a strict diet. The one thing that did give cause for concern, and was relayed to Pat and Hutton in the same message, was that the patient's mental state was quite low: he was described as having resigned himself to his fate. Of concern to the centre's staff was the fact that he was losing his fighting spirit and was developing a 'could not care less attitude', all of which would have an adverse effect on his treatment.

'Poor old Crabbie,' were Pat Rose's thoughts. 'After all that he had been through, the war, the job when he was captured, the brainwashing. He had to spend all those years in Russia, away from all of his friends, and now he had finished with the diving and was, he hoped, being allowed to live in Italy, where he still might not be allowed to meet anybody. He would know that the Russians would watch him day and night and that he would be hounded by the Western press.'

'Now he's ill and needs to fight, what has he left to fight for, poor old Crabbie? Could we get a message to him to tell him we are waiting?' she asked Hutton. He told her that messages were not easy to pass on and the risks were too great, it was far easier to get information out.

The next report stated that Crabb had been assigned a psychoanalyst as a member of the medical team treating him. It was said that he was not aware that he was receiving psychiatric treatment for it was felt that he would have rebelled against it.

Further reports were slow to come and it was not until October 1977 that the next one arrived, passing on the latest information on Crabb's condition. He had responded to treatment and was reported to be as well as could be expected with such an illness. Regarding his mental attitude, the message said that he did not speak to anyone and took no interest in any community activities. 'He keeps himself to himself and frequently sits in an armchair, staring seemingly "unseeing" into the distance. His thoughts are lost to himself.'

That was the last report that Hutton received from his sources behind the Iron Curtain, for he himself died. As far as is known there was nothing sinister about his death, for he had been in poor health for some time. But for us the Crabb saga did not end there.

We had developed a keen desire to visit the grave in Milton Cemetery, which bore the name of Commander Crabb, where the body that had been washed ashore was buried.

Milton Cemetery is a large place and we had entered the office to ask the location of the grave. We were shown a map and direction to the row. The staff at the cemetery had obviously encountered many other visitors to the grave as they had no need to check the records.

Standing on a clear bright day beside the declared grave, we looked at the headstone. It was stark in its whiteness and neither of us drew any feelings from being there. There was a cold, empty atmosphere. We reflected upon who was buried in the plot, if indeed a body was in the coffin at all, and, if there was, whether it was Commander Crabb, or some unknown person used as a cover up.

Whilst we stood at the graveside we became aware that we were being watched, but ignored the observer because for us it was a time for reflection. Mrs Beatrice Crabb, Commander Crabb's mother, had attended the funeral, but never returned for she did not in her heart believe that her son Lionel was buried there. She had been told that the body found was his, but she never really believed the authorities. Pat Rose had not visited the grave upon her return from France, nor in the ensuing years, and she only went in later years out of curiosity. Sydney Knowles told me recently that he did not attend the funeral and that he had not visited the grave, in fact he had not even bothered to learn its location in Portsmouth, for he knew that it was not the body of Commander Crabb buried there. He repeated that he had worked with Crabbie for 13 years and had a great deal of respect for the man, so if he had known that the grave was his, he would have visited it and attended the funeral.

On our visit only the headstone remained, for the stone surround had been removed. We knew that a woman had had the grave maintained over the years, having arranged for bulbs to be planted twice a year. Her identity only emerged later.

As we left the grave, we saw the observer leave the shelter of a group of trees, where he had been standing watching us, and making his way back to the cemetery office. It was obvious that the cemetery staff had been directed to keep a record of visitors to the grave.

The following day we made a telephone call to the cemetery office to ask why the stone surround had been removed, leaving only the headstone. It was explained that as part of a general 'tidy-up' of the cemetery, all additions to graves were being removed, providing permission was given by the owner. This was being done to aid general maintenance and grass cutting. A letter to the owner of Commander Crabb's declared grave had been sent in 1974 asking if any objections would be raised if the headstone was moved to bring it in line with others in the row, and if the stone surround could be removed permanently. Permission was granted and in 1976 the headstone was moved and the stone surround removed. Maintenance of the grave, and the placement of flowers by the unknown woman, continued.

We sought to identify the woman who owned the grave and asked Pat Rose. She replied in a firm voice that it was certainly not herself, 'for there was no point, Crabbie was not buried there.' So she had nothing to do with it. We asked her who she thought the 'woman' was.

'Probably the wife or mother of some poor soul whose body was grabbed by MI5 to be used, as being the body of Crabbie,' she replied.We asked her about Hutton's theory that the body had been planted from a Russian submarine.

'Seems a bit far-fetched to me, no, wouldn't be surprised if it wasn't MI5 or some organisation.'

We then asked her if she had ever visited the grave. She told us, 'Being ill with cancer I had to attend Portsmouth Hospital for treatment. Now the hospital is opposite Milton Cemetery and one of the nurses asked me if I had ever seen the grave. I told her that I hadn't and explained the reason why. She then said, "Wouldn't you like to have a look out of curiosity?" and I told her, "No". The matter raised itself again and she said that she would come with me, so I agreed. We went over and, like yourselves, went to the office to find out where it was, for neither of us had been there before. Standing by the headstone, it meant nothing to me, for I knew that Crabbie was not there, and I felt bitter that they had dear old Crabbie's name on a headstone and they knew it wasn't his body and that he wasn't dead.

She paused to regain herself, then continued, 'As we were leaving the cemetery one of the men said to us that he had seen us at Commander Crabb's grave. I told him that the Commander was not buried there, and he agreed, and told us that he knew that Commander

Crabb was not buried there.' She paused again, then said, 'Everybody connected with the grave or the inquest knows that the body, if, as you say, there even is a body buried there, is not Crabbie'.

We had a photograph of the original grave, and laid it beside the photograph that we had taken on our visit. We were looking at the differences with the stone surround removed. Then Jackie exclaimed that it was not the same headstone. We looked carefully at the photographs, comparing the details. The original photograph showed the headstone as being dirty and displaying the stains of weathering which had left marks running from the words of the inscription. The headstone in the photograph that we had taken was new, sparkling and with no weathering stains. We had been looking for something obvious and not something radical, for as we analysed the photographs we found that not only was the headstone new and clean, but the inscription was different. It had been altered. Crabb's mother originally had the headstone inscribed:

IN
EVER LOVING MEMORY
OF
MY SON
COMMANDER CRABB
AT REST AT LAST

This was a very strange epitaph from a mother to a son as it omitted his Christian names, naval service, decorations and date. She placed that inscription, she confided to friends, 'because they say it's my son Lionel in there but I don't believe them.' She went to her grave never knowing the truth.

The new headstone read:

IN
LOVING MEMORY
OF MY SON
COMMANDER
LIONEL CRABB
RNVR GM OBE
AT REST AT LAST
1956

The next telephone call to the cemetery office was to enquire about the change of the headstone. We were told that it had been removed in February 1982 to be cleaned, re-inscribed and replaced. However, the task of re-inscribing would have been a considerable one for the extra words could not have been fitted in, the face would have had to be made smooth first, then the complete text inscribed. Alternatively a new headstone could have been made. The work was done at the express wishes and expense of the present owner, the unknown woman, and the cemetery staff had to remain silent as to the identity of the owner of the grave.

A woman, whom it seemed nobody could find, had paid for the flowers to be planted on the grave and then for the headstone to be altered. We assumed that it was one and the same person. If we couldn't find the owner, then we would find the stone mason who undertook the commission.

In 1981, Barrells of Portsmouth were commissioned to remove the headstone from Milton Cemetery and take it to their workshops, where the face was skimmed off and the remainder of the stone cleaned. They then re-inscribed the sparkling white stone with the new inscription. It was taken back to the cemetery and replaced on the grave.

Who made the commission and why? The answer – which we finally discovered through luck and good detective work – emerged as banal! The woman was a cousin of Crabb's, whose name had never before been mentioned. She had been close to Beatrice Crabb, his mother, and after her death took over the responsibility of looking after the grave.

The family was told that the body was *presumed* to be that of Commander Crabb, and, even though the coroner's court was given no firm evidence that it was his remains which had been found, a death certificate was issued. No member of Crabb's family was called upon to identify the remains, though, which is very strange. Even his mother was never asked to look at the body, and she would certainly have known about his toe deformity and could have made a useful contribution to the vital identification process.

Crabb's cousin made an arrangement with the cemetery officials to have the grave maintained, by having flowers planted twice a year.

She never visited the grave and all communication was undertaken by post.

In 1981, the 25th anniversary of Crabb's disappearance, there was renewed interest in the grave, so much so that the cemetery authorities wrote to the woman to say that they had received numerous enquiries about who was maintaining the grave; however, they had refused to pass on any information. We have been informed by the woman's son that, also in 1981, she was contacted by an unnamed visitor and as a result of that meeting caused the headstone to be re-inscribed. Why she did this and who the visitor was we shall never know, for Crabb's cousin has since died at the age of 87.

12

Further Evidence

During 1987 the controversial book *Spycatcher*, written by Peter Wright, a former MI5 mole hunter, became available outside the United Kingdom. Within its pages Wright delves into various investigations into high-level penetration of the secret service by Russian agents. The Crabb affair is described as MI6's biggest débâcle and yet only gains a mere page of irrelevant information. Crabb's operation was and still is taboo. When we wrote to Chapman Pincher about it, he told us that a security service officer who knew more about the Crabb operation had written some memoirs but had been strictly forbidden to mention the Crabb incident.

One aspect of Crabb's disappearance which had concerned us throughout our research was how the Russians knew what he was doing during the post-war years when he moved from the Royal Navy to MI6 and then back to the Navy before returning to MI6. His was an involved and complex role, especially as far as the intricacies of diving were concerned. It would have needed a special knowledge and the key to the puzzle could have come from one man: Professor J.B.S. Haldane. Involved with the Admiralty Underwater Experimental Unit during World War Two in the development of human torpedoes and midget submarines, he undertook valuable experimental work in the physiology of diving, especially the effects of breathing pure oxygen underwater. After the war he remained in experimental diving and undertook research into deep-sea diving techniques, leading to Britain's obtaining the world record from a deep dive. He would without doubt have known Crabb and the relevance lies in the damning statement in Wright's book that Haldane was supplying all details of the diving experiments to the Communist Party of Great Britain who in turn passed them on to the GRU in London. It takes little imagination to speculate that details about Crabb's activities could have taken the same route.

There has also been much speculation about Crabb's state of health prior to the dive on the *Ordzhonikidze*. We had extensive interviews with a respected former Royal Marine Special Boat Squadron officer, who coincidentally was the son of Crabb's old friend Maitland Pendock. He knew Crabb during the 1950s, and the work he was involved with, and provided the following evidence.

Crabb's role in the Navy during the early 1950s revolved around secret underwater work, including the development of specialised, purpose-made miniature demolition devices for the disposal of bombs and mines without having to resort to total demolition. He was also very interested in the development of underwater mini-submarines and swimmer vehicles. He worked with the Royal Marines Special Boat Squadron teams in developing techniques for covert operations, but a cloak of secrecy lay, and lies, over their work. Despite his age he was physically fit; he was skilled in the art of locking out of and back into submarines whilst they were submerged and had been part of a team that attempted to penetrate a Russian naval base to undertake a secret underwater operation, having been taken there and collected by a submerged submarine (an operation also described by Pat Rose earlier in the book).

Within the organisation that gathered the naval intelligence, Crabb a Commander, RN, was fairly junior in rank, but was always regarded with respect and some awe by those his senior.

The covert operations undertaken by the SBS even thirty years ago are not discussed, or even hinted at, so adding fuel to the inevitable question as to whether Crabb would have been a worthwhile prize for the Russians at that period. The answer must be positive, and those who really knew what he was doing up to the time he disappeared agree that his knowledge and experience would have been of the highest value to the Soviet Union – but only for a limited number of years. Developments and advances in the underwater aspects of warfare were coming so swiftly that his knowledge of British methods would have become outdated, but he could have continued to undertake trials and command diving teams, all of which would have been useful. The Russians could also have used him for political bargaining.

We have consistently maintained that Crabb was grabbed by the Russians in their determined efforts to develop a large number of underwater swimmers. In the 1950s SCUBA diving as a sport was virtually non-existent anywhere in the world, but especially in the USSR. Then, in the space of three years, the 'sport' of SCUBA diving was developed. It was in late 1956 that the first section in the USSR Central Sea Club (CSC) was opened for the training of SCUBA divers, and courses were soon established for underwater swimmers and instructors. An English article in a Soviet magazine explained that other sections were established in Leningrad, Sevastopol, Odessa and Vladivostok, as well as other cities. The fact that this major event happened 'instantly' in 1956, and involved all the places where Crabb is reported to have served, is suspicious. Evidence discussed earlier also describes the formation of the élite *Spetsnaz* combat swimmer battalions in 1956. Coincidence or conspiracy?

In fact it is not uncommon for the Russians to use covert means to gain control of something they want: we need look no further than the *United States Missing in Action* (MIAs) statistics from the South East Asia war. Recent reports state that many of the back-seat technicians of sophisticated aircraft and ground radar technicians were classed as MIA, MB (*Missing in Action, Moscow Bound*). The Russians wanted information on advanced airborne electronic and radar systems, especially '*counter*' developments, and they were able to spirit those men they wanted away.

A curious twist in the saga takes us back to the bodies found in the waters off the south coast in 1956 and 1957, both of which were dressed in rubber diving suits. Investigators disagreed as to whether the body was planted by the Soviet GRU or by some British agency, but there might conceivably have been *two* bodies, planted in ignorance of each other by both sides in order to put an end to the speculation over Commander Crabb's disappearance.

In an interview with Mike O'Meara, a friend of the authors and a formal naval clearance diver, Harry Cole recalled in detail how he found a body in 1956, only a few months after the furore in Portsmouth and London.

Harry comes from a family of fisherfolk with some 400 years' fishing experience in the Emsworth area, and at the age of 67 he is still actively fishing. He recalls that he was trawling at about 19:00 hours on a dark and windy November evening outside Emsworth Harbour, near Chichester, on his boat, the *Raven*. The aft deck was well lit, a fact which had not been apparent earlier, and the boat was pitching and rolling in the choppy seas. When he hauled in the twelve-foot beam trawl Cole saw a body well tangled within the wing of the trawl board. In unfavourable weather conditions he struggled to free the body which was dressed in frogman's equipment. He gripped with both hands two concertina 'breathing tubes' which passed over either shoulder and around the back of the diver's neck, to connect into a rubber bag.

Unable to move the body he reached and felt a belt which was around the waist. He remembers feeling a square slab weight attached to it. Heaving on the belt, he realised that it was strong but could not say whether it was made of leather or rubberised canvas. Despite what he had said earlier, he now stated that he had never observed nor felt any bottles or canisters.

The body, particularly the face, was covered in prawns, and the parts of the face visible were black and so no identification was possible. The suit, apart from the prawns, was covered in a white/grey substance which when scraped came away to reveal black rubber underneath.

He twisted the body in an attempt to get it into the boat, and the head came away, to fall and sink below the water's surface. Unable to do anything with the body because of the weather, he let it sink into the murky depths, retaining the only evidence in the form of a single corrugated rubber hose, with the mouthpiece.

He did not immediately report his gruesome find to the authorities, for fishermen have a view that what the sea takes it should keep. The item he had recovered from the body was put in a corner of his shed, and the matter died until Harry found an eight-foot dinghy in February 1957, from the yacht *Duessa* which had been wrecked on the West Wittering sands. The yacht was on charter to Lord Upton, who was believed lost at sea.

Harry reported his find to the police, and at the same time told them of the incident from the previous November when he found the body. Details were given to an inspector and a sergeant of the

West Sussex police in Chichester. They did not log details of his *finding and loss of the body*, and were visibly not interested. They did take details of the dinghy.

No action was taken, even though Cole possessed an item of diving equipment which at that period of time was not readily available. He was not visited by the police for further questioning nor by the Navy, nor by anybody from the security services, all of which were well aware that a frogman had gone missing. Yet the item of equipment recovered could have been of vital importance in the possible identification.

Harry received a letter together with a cheque for £5 from the Receiver of Wrecks Portsmouth dated 22 February 1957. No mention was made about the body or item of apparatus that he had recovered.

He did ask the police to come and examine the hose and mouthpiece, but they were not interested. He also warned them that a headless body would be found in the near future within Emsworth harbour.

Because of the lack of interest by the Chichester police, he reported it to his local Emsworth police constable, an officer called Brown. The officer reassured Harry that he had done all that was required of him by informing the Chichester police.

After a body was recovered by John Randall and the Gilbys, Detective Superintendent Hoare visited Harry with regard to his earlier find. By now the vital physical evidence had been thrown away; Harry was not asked to make a formal statement nor attend the inquest to add what would have been most valuable evidence in the attempted identification process.

What is of interest is the statement made to the inquest that the police officer had made enquiries from all the police forces of the south coast about missing frogmen, yet the find by Harry Cole was never mentioned.

Our own interest now centred on the unusual twin hose 'breathing set' which we wanted to identify. Harry was shown a photograph of a naval issue Clearance Divers Breathing Apparatus (CDBA), which has ball weights and a single breathing hose. He was positive that this was not the same equipment. The counterlung (breathing bag) was not on the chest but around the neck.

Harry was then shown a photograph of Dunlop closed-circuit equipment, which was of Second World War vintage and had twin hoses going down from the mouth over the shoulder to attach to the breathing bag. He said that it was very similar to the equipment which the body had been wearing. He went on to explain that the breathing bag was higher up around the neck.

Neither of us could determine the origin of the equipment. I telephoned Siebe Gorman, who during and after the war were principal designers and manufacturers of closed-circuit breathing apparatus. The only help they could provide was to refer me to their Salvus ANS and Amphibian MK11 apparatus of Second World War vintage. These had breathing bags that fitted around the neck, but, from evidence provided by Harry, these were not the same as that worn by the body he found.

I telephoned Syd Knowles and described the equipment to him, and he recalled that there was apparatus answering that description around at the time. He could not recall whether it was of Italian origin. Another source said that the Italians did have equipment of that description.

We raised with Harry the subject of the ball weights which we had been told had been seen by an investigator. Harry categorically stated that there were no ball weights, he never saw or recovered any. The only item he salvaged was one hose of a pair which had the mouthpiece attached.

It is fair to presume that 'they' wanted a body to be found, but with only pieces of rubber and bone remaining so as to make identification impossible. Did the second body found by Randall come from Russia or was it the first, found by Cole, free of entanglement, and floating on the tide? The latter assumption would discredit Hutton's account of the body's being prepared in Russia and released from one of their submarines, which was deemed credible by the support provided by Sir Percy Sillitoe, the former director of MI5.

Why did the British authorities do absolutely nothing about Harry Cole's dramatic find, or his irrefutable physical evidence? And why, when the second body was found, was Cole not taken to inspect the remains, in order to assist in the identification?

The mystery surrounding the Crabb affair could have ended on 1 January 1987 when the Cabinet Papers for 1956 became available to the public under the thirty year rule. But nothing was forthcoming, and, through the lack of any evidence, the authorities have in effect admitted that the Crabb affair had deeper implications than many people had supposed.

The information released in a single file, titled the 'Death of Crabb', provided no new evidence about the operation, but merely showed how the various departments coped with the fiasco as it evolved. The other files containing the vital evidence were not available and were not to be made public even after thirty years.

The Times on 1 January 1987 recorded the event with a small article, headlined, 'Veil stays on the Crabb Spying Episode.'

'The mystery of frogman Commander Lionel "Buster" Crabb who was involved in an unauthorised spying operation on Soviet warships in Portsmouth harbour in 1956 will not be completely unravelled for at least another 70 years.' The article continued to say that the Government has decided not to allow the Cabinet papers about Crabb to be released under the thirty year rule, but has decided to keep the file with the most sensitive records closed until the year 2057.

Other newspapers followed with similar references to the lack of information released about the incident that is to remain *officially* untold for 100 years.

13

Karlovy Vary

The Ilyushin I1-62 of Czechoslovak Airlines made a smooth touch-down at Prague's Ruzyne airport and taxied to park amidst other aircraft of both Czechoslovakia and the Soviet airline Aeroflot. It was October 1987, and a mysterious series of events had taken us to Czechoslovakia where we hoped to find and fit the final part of the Commander Crabb jigsaw. Pat Rose had died in January of that year, but we determined to find out what had become of her 'Crabbie'. It was, for us, by far the most dangerous part of our investigations into the Crabb affair, for it entailed a cloak and dagger journey behind the Iron Curtain to meet and speak with people we did not know, and who would not identify themselves.

All evidence had pointed to Crabb – Korablov being at a medical institute in the town of Karlovy Vary, which is in a country where everyday freedoms are restricted and where foreigners cannot go and ask questions regarding the whereabouts of a Russian naval officer. In November 1986 we had written to the state medical centre at Karlovy Vary to enquire about the fate of a Russian naval officer, Commander Lev Lvovich Korablov who was reported to have been at the centre in 1977 – 88. We did not receive a reply, nor did we really expect one, as such a letter would have found its way to the desk of the relevant security service for recording and filing.

It was many months later when I answered the telephone that the letter resurfaced. The voice at the other end of the phone asked to speak to Mr Welham. A strong East European accent made a poor pronunciation of my name, but I informed the male voice that he was speaking to Mr Welham. He asked if I was seeking information about a Russian naval officer called Korablov and why I wanted such information. It took some moments for the question to sink in as the call was totally unexpected. I asked who was speaking but the question was ignored, the man simply repeating the same question again. I responded that I was interested to know about the man as my wife and I were writing a book about a former Royal Navy officer who had disappeared, and we thought that they were one and the same. There was a pause at the other end of the phone, then the voice said that the Russian officer Korablov was the Englishman and that he had been a 'swimmer underwater' in both navies. I was stunned by the words, for we had heard Pat Rose tell us of such telephone calls, and like her shared an anxiety as to its validity. I again asked who the person was and why should I believe what he said, for it could have been an elaborate hoax. In a slow guttural tone he explained that within Czechoslovakia there are anti-Russian movements who stand for various causes, such as religious and speech freedoms, while others such as his own group wanted to expose the sinister aspects of the Russian presence within their country. Although they had little information on Crabb – Korablov they wanted to tell us what they did know. They could have told us over the telephone what we wanted to hear, but explained that if we were prepared to go to Karlovy Vary then they would arrange for us to meet someone who had known Crabb in the sanatorium, and we could see the sanatorium where he was a patient. A million questions raced through my mind but the man finished by saying that we would be contacted again, then the phone went dead.

The next phone call was answered by Jackie who had great difficulty in understanding the woman who had called, because of her strong East European accent. She wanted to know if we were going to make the journey, and was pleased when Jackie confirmed that we were. She explained that we did not have any travel details yet and asked how we could get in touch when they were confirmed. The woman would give no name, telephone number or address, but said that she would contact us again. Jackie gave her our planned visit dates, but much depended upon flights and hotels. Jackie also took the opportunity to ask if the woman was talking about the same person whom we sought, to which the woman replied that Korablov had been an English Navy man, and concluded by saying that she would contact us again.

We had also been in contact with a former citizen of Czechoslovakia who now resided in Britain. He was most helpful in explaining about the system of control within the country and the best way to conduct ourselves. I did not tell him about our telephone calls, but said that in search of information we were going to Karlovy Vary. He knew some details of the Crabb affair and considered it perfectly natural that the Russians would grab somebody they wanted and then dump them in a satellite country when they had finished with them. It was explained in detail, many times, that Czechoslovakia is a total police state and has an efficient security service linked to the KGB. The people could move about the country as they pleased, but to travel outside was a different matter. 'Glasnost' as preached by Mikhail Gorbachov to the West was a sham, and the people were controlled and oppressed. If we sought information about a Czech citizen, that was one thing, but to enquire about a Russian naval officer, who would have been under the control of the GRU, was quite another matter.

I gave him details of our travel arrangements with the understanding that he would do what he could to arrange help in Karlovy Vary.

The final phone call from the anonymous woman was brief and to the point. We gave her details of our visit, and she laid down one major ground rule: the people in Karlovy Vary would contact us and we were not to photograph them or do anything that could put them at risk. We naturally accepted the conditions. We were to travel as tourists and not as investigative journalists. In the event of an unpleasant situation arising we could get away with being inquisitive English, but the people we would meet could face very long prison sentences. There was the added factor that enquiring in detail about a Russian military person would be considered spying.

We descended the steps from the aircraft and followed fellow passengers to the airport buildings. Upon entering we joined the inevitable queue, and were eventually confronted by a poker-faced uniformed official who looked at our passports and visas; handing them back he nodded for us to proceed. We had already seen the woman standing nearby holding a card with our name on it. After we introduced ourselves, she took us to one side and examined our passports and visas, and used a rubber stamp in the corner of our visas. She said that we should go through the principal passport control, collect our luggage and after passing through customs she would be waiting for us. Was this tour guide efficiency or the rebirth of our letter to the medical institute? We had not been booked an organised tour holiday, so we suspected the latter. Passport control and customs were serviced by dour surly-faced uniformed officials who examined our visas and the mark, before making their official stamp with no questions or demands.

Entering the arrivals hall we saw many people waiting for fellow travellers as well as placard-carrying tour guides, each wearing a small badge with the name of the guide and organisation printed on. Our guide came over to us, now devoid of the card bearing our name and giving no identification as to who she was or what she represented. A taxi awaited, to transport us to the bus station, most unexpected. Jackie and I followed the woman, who was aged about 35, slim and about 5ft 4in tall with longish brown hair. She spoke good English, but never gave away any details about herself. Jackie and I had already named her 'Tinkerbelle'.

Outside the airport building our guide told us that we would have a two-hour wait for the bus, then a journey of two and a half hours: but if we were interested the taxi driver would take us directly to Karlovy Vary and she would return us the bus fare which was pre-paid, and seats reserved. The cost was a figure which we could hardly refuse. Accepting her extremely generous offer we followed her to a taxi, not one of the very common Skodas, but an estate car. The driver spoke very good English also, a fact which we later found to be uncommon. We got into the back and were more than surprised when the guide also got into the car. We were now on full alert as we began an hour's car journey to the town of Karlovy Vary.

As the car sped along a virtually traffic-free road, 'Tinkerbelle' told us all about the virtues of the socialist system, intermingling her commentary with questions about why we were going to Karlovy Vary for such a short time, and whether either of us had been ill? Why didn't we stay in Prague as did most tourists, especially in the autumn? Apart from the general questions came those of a more direct and searching nature: did we know anybody in Karlovy Vary or any Czech people in Britain? What work did we do? That was a question of interest for I said diving, not elaborating any further. Using the English word to a foreigner who is not familiar with the subject, one normally receives a shrug and a request for further explanation. 'Tinkerbelle' immediately asked Jackie about the dangers as if it were a subject she knew a lot about. At no time in any of our tourist visa forms or in conversation had the subject of diving or underwater swimming been earlier raised. 'Tinkerbelle' knew, and she could only have one source of information, the Czech secret service.

Nothing more was said on the subject and only things of a general nature were discussed. Did she know that we suspected her? The next surprise was totally unexpected and occurred as we entered the town of Karlovy Vary. The road follows a twisting route down into a valley and we came across a view of one of the large and grand sanatoria. 'Tinkerbelle' turned to face us, as the car slowed down. She told us that the building was the sanatorium Imperial and was specially for the Russians. She watched our faces, but gained no ground for we mearly nodded acceptance of the information and looked around to other buildings. The car stopped at the Grand Hotel Moskva, whereupon 'Tinkerbelle' said that she would go to the local travel office and tell them that we had arrived. She bade us goodbye.

We checked in at the hotel reception, to be registered by the most surly, unhelpful girl imaginable, totally devoid of any civility. Papers duly signed and stamped, she ordered us to the porter's desk. The porter had been to the same school of charm, and gave us a key without any comment, leaving us to find the room.

Accepting that the rooms were fitted with listening devices to record our conversation, we said very little, and soon took our first look at the town of Karlovy Vary, exchanging thoughts on the car journey. The travel office was not far from the hotel and as we suspected was closed and in darkness, with a steel-barred gate ensuring security. 'Tinkerbelle' had handed us over to the local security department, a fact borne out about an hour later as we slowly walked back to the hotel, looking in shop windows. Jackie observed the 'taxi' which had brought us, and when the occupants realised that we had seen them the car sped past us, 'Tinkerbelle' and the driver ignoring us. But the passenger in the back was more than interested in us, though we watched the car disappear from sight and did not see it again until we got off the bus at Prague station on our return journey.

The following morning found a light mist hanging in the tree-covered hills and after breakfast in our room we explored the town. Karlovy Vary lies in a deep valley where two rivers, the Tepla and the Ohre, converge. The hills that surround the town create a picturesque scene of old and modern buildings, which make it one of the best-known and beautiful of Europe's spas. In the centre of the town is the thermal spring called Vridlo, where the hot waters gush from the earth's interior. These healing waters are warmed to 72 degrees centigrade and spout as high as ten metres. The deep water is warmed underground and mixed with carbon dioxide under pressure. On its way to the surface the water dissolves minerals held in the rocks, which enrich it. The springs have for centuries been used for medicinal purposes, especially internal organ treatment. It soon became evident that people came not only for extended periods of treatment but to visit for a few hours, having travelled as a bus party.

To gain a grandstand view of the sanatorium Imperial we made our way towards a conical-roofed viewing point on the hillside, directly opposite. Autumn was in full flight as we climbed the railed and marked footpath, walking on a carpet of golden brown and yellow leaves. We shared the climb with other visitors and possibly members of the Czech secret service, to eventually stand in the observation point which revelled in the exotic name of Mayeruv Gloriet. It was built in grander days, of a round wooden construction with a conical roof. A bench seat follows the shape, allowing the observer to sit and recover after the climb and look out over the town. When a group of visitors departed the spot, we proceeded to photograph the panorama before us, especially the sanatorium Imperial, which was brought in to close and stark relief with a telephoto lens.

Neither of us saw or heard the man approach, he just seemed to appear. Hearing us speak, he asked us, in the heavily accented voice with which were becoming very familiar, if we were English. When we said we were, he looked across at the Imperial and told us straight out that we were looking at the place where Korablov had been. It was what we had come to hear but, out on that hillside in a strange country, it made the small hairs on the back of the neck stand up.

We didn't respond to the statement but continued to look at the distant building and the man. He was just over six feet tall, with greying hair, swept back to emphasise his receding hair line. A heavy set frame filled the brown leather jacket, and his facial features seemed to us to be typically Czech: he was one of the crowd, never standing out, but blending with those around him. He gave us no name, and it was again made clear that neither he, nor anybody he was with, must be photographed for the risk of identification was too great and they would face severe prison sentences after the KGB had finished with them.

The ground rules laid, he told us that Korablov was a Russian naval officer who was in fact English. They had known this for a long time but, as nobody had sought to enquire, they could not divulge the information. Jackie asked how they found out about us, to which he only said that the anti-Russian movement had people sympathetic to the cause in many places, including buildings.'We found you, that is all you need to know.' We told him about 'Tinkerbelle', but that merely produced a shrug of the shoulders and the bland comment that we had to be careful. The thought that crossed our minds later was the realisation that we had been speaking about a Russian military officer to a complete stranger, within the Soviet stronghold. The main question on our part was, how did they know that Korablov was the man we sought?

A woman who had worked at the sanatorium and looked after the man would talk to us and tell us what she knew. We would then see that the Russian and English naval officer were the same. Two other questions were on our minds, the first being: if he had died at the Imperial where was he buried? Was he laid to rest in the town's graveyard? It was explained that the Russians brought people to the Sanatorium, that most recovered but that, if anyone should die, the body would be returned to Russia. We would find no graves of Russians in Karlovy Vary. We asked whether, since Crabb was of the Roman Catholic faith, the Church would have any information? The man answered by telling us that Russian naval officers would not be allowed to display any religious convictions, especially in front of the Czech staff.

The arrangements for meeting the woman were that we should visit the J. Gargarin Colonnade each day at 11 am and wait for one hour.

If nothing happened then we would return at 2 pm and again wait for one hour. Doing this would be perfectly natural and would establish a pattern for anybody watching us. The colonnade is a long modern building where five pillars deposit healing waters from the thermal springs and visitors or patients can fill cups and drink and relax. The times we were told to be there were the busiest and, with the entire building full of people milling about, it was a very suitable place to arrange a meeting. The man's parting message was simple and clear, they would contact us, we were to wait and be patient. He disappeared as quickly as he had arrived; our link with the anti-Russian movement was made.

Although we were not followed openly, we were certainly watched, especially in the town. The same person would arrive in a café or shop as we tracked and back-tracked our way through the streets. Whenever we passed the colonnade, it provided an excuse to enter, sit and sample the warm waters. The hotel reception would have nothing to do with us, and the only response we got was to be directed to the porter's desk. The porters in turn, although speaking English, gave a guarded response to every question we asked. One incident of note occurred after I had procured a Czech magazine on swimming and SCUBA diving. Approaching the porter who I knew spoke the best English, I placed the magazine before him. I pointed to the photographs, one of the swimmers underwater, and the other of a diver in SCUBA equipment on land. The shock was clearly visible on his face and he stepped back, saying nothing. When I rephrased my initial question about diving in Czechoslovakia, he only looked at the pictures, became very furtive and looked about for an excuse to leave. Another guest entered the hotel and approached the desk giving the porter his opportunity to leave and ignore me. It was after that incident that we were followed in the classic manner: when we stopped, the 'tail' stopped.

The travel company who had shown such concern through 'Tinkerbelle' had no interest in us at the town's office. The staff, who spoke English, albeit not fluently, attempted to answer all questions, but when I enquired about the Sanatorium Imperial, they said that they did not speak English.

Sanatorium Imperial was set in open park-type grounds. There was no security wall nor guards, and we took the opportunity to gain a close look at Crabb's last known home. It was a large, well-kept building, the product of a bygone era. A large notice written in Czech, Russian, English and German demanded that every visitor must report to the reception. The reception was centred at the front and all other doors were firmly closed, displaying the 'go to reception' notice. Many of the lower level windows had bars: we did not know if they were designed to keep people in or out. As we moved freely around the grounds I photographed the building, but Jackie felt uneasy and wanted to move away. The place gave her a feeling which she found hard to describe, as if thousands of unseen eyes were watching us, guarding one of its secrets.

The colonnade was full of people, different nationalities, cultures and social status mingling around the water spouts. A high hubbub of noise was produced by a number of languages, all merging together. We sat on the seats which surrounded the glass-windowed walls and watched the flow of people and sipped the warm mineral water. The feeling of exposure, even in such a crowded place, crept over us as we became aware of the man who stood close by us. He wore the same clothes as on our first encounter. Neither party acknowledged the other, but it was obvious that, if the woman was to be here, it was to be a well timed and chosen spot, for nobody could overhear our conversation, or record or photograph the meeting. All parties could, if danger approached, move off to mingle in the crowd and become 'lost'. A woman, who blended perfectly with the general mêlée, moved up to sit beside us, sipping the waters from her newly purchased cup. She asked us in English if we liked the water and were enjoying our stay. We had met the contact, the person who had been with Crabb in his last days and who was to satisfy us that it was not his body in the grave at Portsmouth.

In her sixties, she had grey hair and was well built, but not excessively. A kind round face made her look matronly, and the clothes added to the impression, even though she was well dressed.

Her story began with the war when, as a young woman, she remembered the German troops and then how they were first 'liberated', and had been controlled ever since, by the Russians. She had been involved with medicine from those early days and because she spoke Russian had eventually got a job at the Sanatorium Imperial, as more and more Russian patients came for treatment. Her involvement with the medical profession had required her to learn English, although she could not remember very much, for it was not used very often. All questions as to what she actually did in the sanatorium were to no avail. She told us that she was employed at the Imperial dealing with Russians, who treated the Czechs as second class citizens (which is, in fact, how the Russians view the situation). The one Russian who was different arrived, as far as she could remember, about Christmas 1977, she could link the date through a personal family happening. He was a small man, who had come to be treated for internal medical problems. In the beginning he was not noticed and she could remember little about him, but recalls that he was polite, which was unusual for a Russian, and did not mix with the other patients. She told us that she did not remember the name she had been told [Korablov] for it was a long time ago and patients came and went, the staff were moved about to limit any familiarity or gathering of information about patients.

The man did not seem to be getting any better, seemingly having lost the will to live, but drugs and the curative treatment prolonged his life. He lost weight and she recalled that it made his nose look larger, and made a sign of a hooked nose. She laughed when explaining about the bushy hair on his cheeks which he flatly refused to allow the barber to shave off. It was grey, as was the thinning hair on his head. He would sit for hours and stare at the distant hills, lost to himself, speaking little and sometimes not at all to some staff. This was the picture conveyed by the woman.

The day he spoke English really surprised her, as she was only one of a very limited number of staff who could understand any of the language. Sometimes a combination of Russian and English confused her, but he trusted her and told her that he was really English. That confused her, for she could not understand what an Englishman was doing as a Russian naval officer, even though she new the Russians to be devious. We asked her if he said anything about England, to which she replied that he told her that he was the only diver to have served in the English Navy and the Russian Navy and to have medals from both. We clarified the word 'diver', to ensure that she understood it: yes, a diver was an underwater swimmer, she knew what a diver was.

We asked her if she reported the fact that he spoke English to anybody else. She explained that some of the Czech staff knew that he spoke a language which she understood, but they did not. At no time did she report the fact to the senior staff, either Czech or Russian, for fear of repercussions.

Did he ever discuss England and any of the people he knew? It was very a important question, but she explained that often he was in pain and when he spoke English she did not always understand what he said; also, she was busy and did not have much time to spend with him.

Every detail she told us about the elderly, grey-haired man, with an emaciated body and a drawn hawkish face, accentuated by the large hook-shaped nose, made us certain that it was Crabb; hearing her description was like listening to Pat Rose again.

The woman told us that for a while she was moved elsewhere in the sanatorium and lost touch, but in 1981 she was transferred back to the section and was very surprised to see that he was still alive. During one of her last short conversations with him he told her that he had been captured by the Russians and made to serve in their Navy. He had waited to go home, by which she thought he meant that the British would take him home.

At no time, in any of our dealings with the organisation, did we provide any details about the Crabb affair, and the only name we ever used was Korablov.

During the latter part of 1981 the woman left Karlovy Vary so she did not have the final answer, but said she thought he must have died. She anticipated our request as to whether any files might be at the sanatorium, and was adamant that all papers on every Russian were kept secure, and left with the patient alive or dead. We assimilated her words, often difficult to hear because of the noise and her accent, but as she was about to leave I thanked her for telling us about Commander Crabb. She looked at us for a moment and asked what was the word I had used. I repeated the 'Crabb'. She told us that was a word he used, but she did not know what it meant. We told her it was his English name. Her parting words before disappearing into the crowd were that she suspected that Crabb died in 1981 –

the year the alterations had been made to Crabb's headstone in Portsmouth. We never saw her again.

The *Daily Mirror* published the following statement shortly after Crabb's disappearance in 1956.

'Frogman Blunder

THE BIG COVER-UP

'One thing is clear from Sir Anthony Eden's House of Commons statement yesterday about the missing frogman:

'This is the Big Cover-Up for a Political Blunder.

'EDEN FLATLY REFUSED TO GIVE MPs ANY REAL INFORMATION!

'The world will now assume that Commander Crabb was sent to spy round the Russian cruiser at a time when Bulganin and Khrushchev were in Britain as guests of the Prime Minister.

'The damage to East-West relations, therefore, has been done.

THE TRUTH CAN DO NO MORE DAMAGE?

OR CAN IT!

For us, the story of Commander Crabb will never die, though there are those who wish that it would . For the Crabb operation has always been a hot potato. Its importance is further borne out by the revelations, released under the thirty year rule on 1 January 1989, regarding two accidents in 1958 at the Windscale plutonium plant (now called Sellafield). During these incidents, strontium 90 was released into the atmosphere to provide readings many times higher than the national average and up to ten times the highest recorded figures for weapon fall-out.

This information has been released amidst the nuclear industry's most difficult period, in the thick of a protest from an expanding anti-nuclear lobby. Why these incidents were not subject to the black hole of time, like the Crabb affair, is perhaps best answered by the fact that the implications surrounding accidents at a plutonium plant were not as serious as those of Crabb's operation.

Bibliography

COMBAT FROGMEN by Michael G. Welham. Patrick Stephens Ltd., 1989.

COMMANDER CRABB by Marshall Pugh. Macmillan & Co. Ltd., 1956.

COMMANDER CRABB IS ALIVE by J. Bernard Hutton. Universal-Tandem Publishing Co. Ltd., 1968.

OPERATION PORTLAND by Harry Houghton. Granada Publishing Ltd., 1972.

THEIR TRADE IS TREACHERY by Chapman Pincher. Sidgwick & Jackson Ltd., 1981.

JANE'S FIGHTING SHIPS. Jane's Publishing Co. Ltd.

A HISTORY OF THE BRITISH SECRET SERVICE by Richard Deacon. Granada Publishing Ltd., 1980.

A MATTER OF TRUST: MI5 1945 – 72 by Nigel West. Weidenfeld & Nicolson, 1982.

TOO SECRET TOO LONG by Chapman Pincher. Sidgwick & Jackson, 1984.

FROGMAN SPY

SOVIET MILITARY INTELLIGENCE by Viktor Suvorov. Grafton Books, 1986.

THE FAKE DEFECTOR by J. Bernard Hutton. Howard Baker Publishers Ltd., 1970.

THE DICTIONARY OF ESPIONAGE by Christopher Dobson & Ronald Payne. Harrap Ltd., 1984.

NTS Introduction to a Russian Freedom Party. Possev, 1979.

Index